AutoCAD® Transition
from 12 to 13

Stephen J. Ethier
Christine A. Ethier
New Brunswick Community College

Prentice Hall

Upper Saddle River, New Jersey   Columbus, Ohio

Cover art/photo: West Light
Editor: Stephen Helba
Production Editor: Patricia S. Kelly
Design Coordinator and Cover Designer: Karrie M. Converse
Production Manager: Laura Messerly
Marketing Manager: Frank Mortimer, Jr.

This book was set in Times Roman and Helvetica by Stephen J. Ethier and Christine A. Ethier and was printed and bound by Courier/Kendallville, Inc. The cover was printed by Phoenix Color Corp.

Brief Contents

CHAPTER 1

Transition

1.1 Introduction

The purpose of this book is to make the transition from release 12 to release 13 as painless as possible. There are several things with which to contend. Not only may you be switching releases but also you may be switching from the DOS version of AutoCAD to the Windows version. This book is laid out so that no matter what path you are taking to move from 12 to 13, you will be able to find your way.

Remember, however, the intent of this book is not to teach you how to use AutoCAD but to assist you to locate the new material in release 13 (R13) and to associate the changes with what you already know about AutoCAD 12 (R12).

The book is logically separated into the various program categories with which the R12 user is already familiar and links them to the changes in R13. Each chapter explains where the associated commands can be found and identifies how they have changed in the new release.

This first chapter presents the R13 screen, in both DOS and Windows, in order to demonstrate any layout changes. Next, the book will explore Viewing and Drawing Aids, Draw, Modify, Text, Dimension, and Solid Modeling

In most cases you will be introduced first to what has changed from R12 to R13 and next to what is different between the DOS and Windows versions.

1.2 Installation

Before R13 of AutoCAD, the DOS and Windows versions were sold separately, and, as such, they were installed separately and placed in separate subdirectories. With R13, both the DOS and Windows versions come together on one CD-ROM. In fact, you have access to both programs as well as the different Windows platforms - Windows 3.1, Windows 95 and Windows NT. To make things simpler, this book will display the Windows graphics from the Windows 3.1 platform and will normally refer to this Windows version as WIN.

When you install AutoCAD R13, whether you install both DOS and Windows versions, or either one or the other, they will be grouped under one subdirectory. This is usually named R13. The R13 subdirectory is subdivided for DOS, WIN, and COM, which is an additional subdirectory that contains files common to both platforms.

1.3 Launching the Program

This section deals with the methods required to launch the AutoCAD program.

DOS

To launch AutoCAD, various settings must first be established. These are usually set before the actual AutoCAD program is run with the use of a batch file. The batch file is created when you first install AutoCAD. The following are the batch files for release 12 and 13 that establish those settings.

Release 12 Batch File: ACADR12.BAT

```
SET ACAD=C:\ACAD12\SUPPORT;C:\ACAD12\FONTS;C:\ACAD12\ADS;C:\ACAD12\SAMPLE
SET ACADCFG=C:\ACAD12
SET ACADDRV=C:\ACAD12\DRV
C:\ACAD12\ACAD %1 %2
```

Release 13 Batch File: ACADR13.BAT

```
SET
ACAD=C:\R13\COM\SUPPORT;C:\R13\DOS;C:\R13\DOS\SUPPORT;C:\R13\COM\FONTS
SET ACADCFG=C:\R13\DOS
SET ACADDRV=C:\R13\DOS\DRV
C:\R13\DOS\ACAD %1 %2
```

As you can see, there is not much difference between the R12 and R13 batch files. The main difference is the location of the subdirectories as mentioned in Section 1.2.

WINDOWS

To launch the Windows version of AutoCAD, you double-pick the appropriate AutoCAD icon from a program group window. Your system may have different types of icons but the following are the typical ones and the program item properties that go with them.

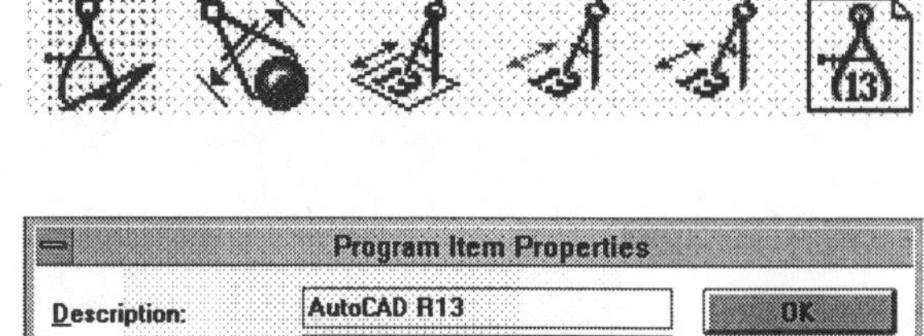

Like the two releases of DOS, the major differences between the two releases of WIN lie in the location of the subdirectories. However, the difference between the WIN version and the DOS version is that the WIN version uses an ACAD.INI file to establish settings instead of the DOS batch file. You can make changes to the ACAD.INI file once AutoCAD has been loaded by selecting the Preferences menu item found under the Options pull-down menu in R13.

1.4 Reviewing the Screen

If you are moving from DOS R12 to DOS R13 you will find that there are very few changes in the screen layout. However, if you are moving from DOS R12 or WIN R12 to WIN R13, you must be prepared for a major change.

DOS

The DOS R12 and DOS R13 screens are very similar. The main difference is the menu groupings and the addition of the workfile size indicator. Refer to Figure 1.1 for an illustration of the R13 screen.

Figure 1.1
DOS ACADR13 screen

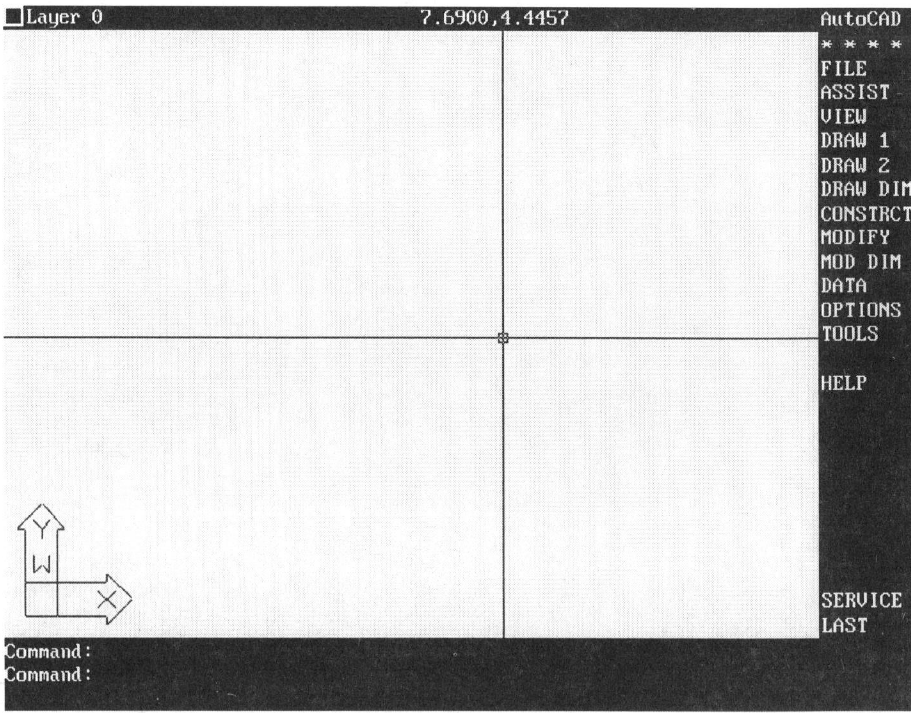

PULL-DOWN MENU

The following is a listing of the R13 pull-down menu headings and the items that fall under each:

File	Assist	View	Draw
New	Undo	Redraw View	Line
Open	Redo	Redraw All	Construction Line
Save	Object Snap	Zoom	Ray
Save As	Point Filters	Pan	Sketch
Print	Snap	Named Views	Polyline
External Reference	Grid	3D Viewpoint Presets	3D Polyline
Bind	Ortho	3D Viewpoint	Multiline
Import	Select Objects	3D Dynamic View	Spline
Export	Selection	Tiled Model Space	Arc
Management	Filters	Floating Model Space	Circle
Exit	Group Objects	Paper Space	Ellipse
	Hatch	Tiled Viewports	Polygon
	Selection	Floating Viewports	Point
	Inquiry	Preset UCS	Insert
	Cancel	Named UCS	Surfaces
		Set UCS	Solids
			Hatch
			Text
			Dimensioning

Construct	Modify	Data	Options
Copy	Properties	Object Creation	Drawing Aids
Offset	Move	Layers	Running Object Snap
Mirror	Rotate	Viewport Layer Controls	Coordinate Display
Array	Align	Color	Selection
Chamfer	Stretch	Linetype	Grips
Fillet	Scale	Multiline Style	UCS
Region	Lengthen	Text Style	Display
Boundary	Point	Dimension Style	Linetypes
Union	Trim	Shape File	Preferences
Subtract	Extend	Units	Configure
Intersection	Break	Drawing Limits	Dialog Box Colors
Block	Edit Polyline	Time	Render Configure
Attribute	Edit Multiline	Status	Tablet
3D Array	Edit Spline	Rename	Log Files
3D Mirror	Edit Text	Purge	Auto Save Time
3D Rotate	Edit Hatch		System Variables
	Attribute		
	Explode		
	Erase		
	Oops!		

Tools	Help
Applicat	Help
Run Script	Search for Help On
External Commands	How to Use Help
Aerial View	What's New in Release 13
External Database	About AutoCAD
Hide	
Shade	
Render	
Slide	
Image	
Spelling	
Calculator	
Menus	
Reinitialize	
Compile	

WINDOWS

The WIN R13 screen has changed drastically from the WIN R12 version. Refer to Figure 1.2 showing the WIN R13 screen. The major change is the addition of individual toolbars that can float about the screen or can be docked at any of the four sides of the screen. As well, the Status line is now a toolbar that is normally docked at the bottom of the screen. However, it can be moved around if desired. You can toggle on/off the various modes such as SNAP and GRID by double-picking on them in the Status Bar. Note that the ESC key is now used to cancel commands in the Windows version of AutoCAD.

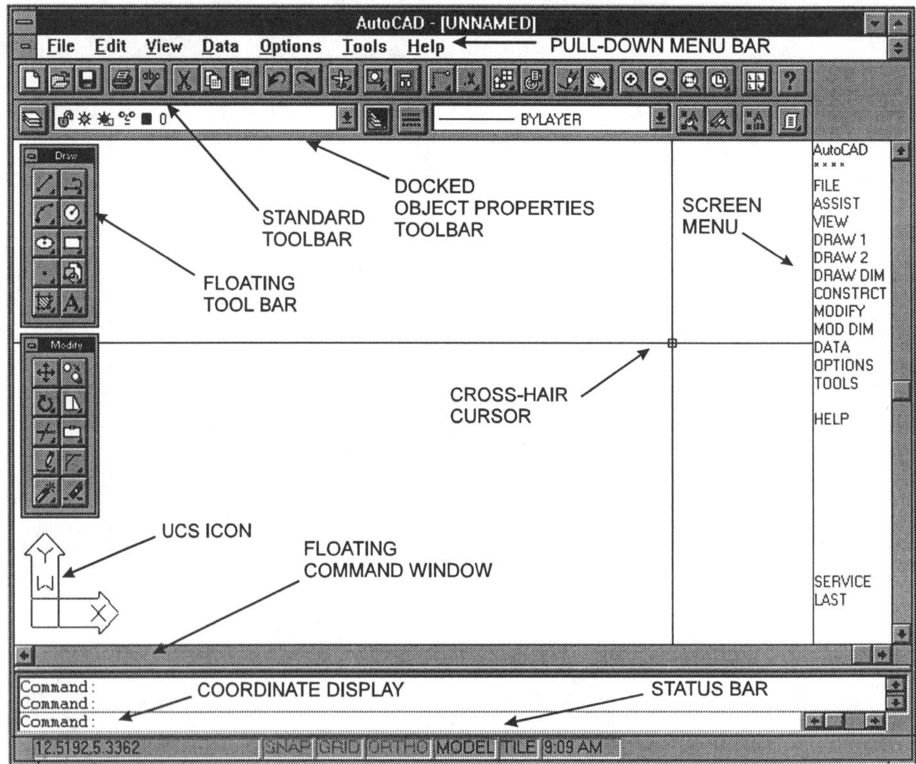

DOCKED TOOLBARS AND FLOATING TOOLBARS

A toolbar is a set of related icons (tools) that pictorially describe a command. They are linked to form a bar. The bar may run horizontally or vertically with single, connected icons or it may float in the form of a rectangle. They are resized by picking on their edges and reshaping them by moving the cursor. Refer to Figure 1.3 for an illustration of different toolbars. The toolbar may float about on the screen or become docked at one of the four sides of the screen. This is done by picking on the edge of the toolbar and dragging it to a new location. Toolbars can be opened from the Tools pull-down menu and they are closed by picking on the minus sign (-) in the upper left corner of the toolbar. Refer to Figure 1.2. Notice the docked Object Properties toolbar that is below the standard toolbar. The Object Properties toolbar controls the appearance of objects drawn on the screen and is a useful toolbar to keep visible and docked.

Tools with a small black triangle have *flyouts* that contain more commands. If you hold down on the pick button, a flyout menu bar is displayed. Figure 1.3 shows the circle flyout under the Draw toolbar. A flyout is similar to a cascading pull-down menu. While holding down on the pick button, you can slide along the flyout selecting other options.

If you move your cursor over a tool icon without picking, a *tooltip* will be displayed. This is a word describing the tool and is accompanied by a line of text on the status line. The display of tooltips can be turned on or off by selecting the Customize Toolbars option from the Tools pull-down menu.

Figure 1.3
Toolbars with flyouts

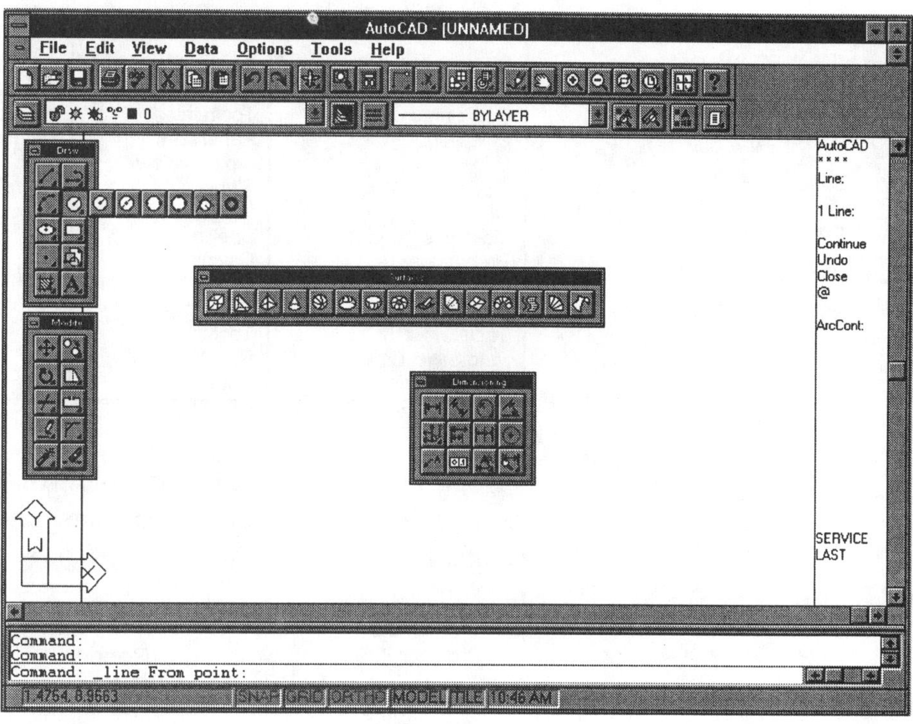

PULL-DOWN MENU

The WIN R13 pull-down menus have not only been given new titles but also have been regrouped. As well, the Draw and Modify pull-down menu items are missing and are now in the form of toolbars. However, a menu that still contains the Draw and Modify pull-down menu items is available for those who desire it. The default menu, ACAD.MNU, has the Draw and Modify pull-down menus removed. However, the ACADFULL.MNU menu file still has the Draw and Modify Menu.

The following is a listing of the pull-down menu headings and the menu items under each one.

File	Edit	View	Data
New	Undo	Redraw View	Object Creation
Open	Redo	Redraw All	Layers
Save	Cut	Zoom	Viewport Layer Control
Save As	Copy	Pan	Color
Save R12 DWG	Copy View	Named Views	Linetype
Print	Paste	3D Viewpoint Presets	Multiline Style
Import	Paste Special	3D Viewpoint	Text Style
Export	Properties	3D Dynamic View	Dimension Style
Options	Links	Tiled Model Space	Shape File
Management	Insert Object	Paper Space	Units
. drawing list .		Tiled Viewports	Drawing Limits
Exit		Floating Viewports	Time
		Preset UCS	Status
		Named UCS	Rename
		Set UCS	Purge

Options	Tools	Help
Drawing Aids	Applications	Contents
Running Object Snap	Run Script	Search for Help on
Coordinate Display	Toolbars	How to Use Help
Selection	Aerial View	What's New in Release 13
Grips	Text Window	Quick Tour
UCS	Slide	Learning AutoCAD
Display	Image	About AutoCAD
Linetypes	Spelling	
Preferences	Calculator	
Configure	Customize Menus	
Render Configure	Customize	
Tablet	Toolbars	
Auto Save Time	Reinitialize	
System Variables	Compile	

You will find that quite a few of the pull-down menu items have been replaced with individual toolbars. The following is a list of individual toolbars:

Draw	Attribute	UCS
Modify	Render	View
Dimensioning	External Database	Object Properties
Solids	Miscellaneous	Standard Toolbar
Surfaces	Selected Objects	
External Reference	Point Filters	

These will be explained in more detail in later chapters.

1.5 Preferences

For those of you new to the Windows version of AutoCAD, R13 makes uses of a Preferences dialog box to make changes to the AutoCAD operating environment. This Preferences command is found under the Options pulldown menu.

In the Windows version, there are five different preferences file folders. The following lists explains these folders:

SYSTEM (Refer to Figure 1.4)

AutoCAD Graphics Window: Controls the display of the screen menu, scroll bars, and window repair.

Automatic Save: Allows you to save your drawing automatically at set intervals. The name of the save file is controlled using the CONFIG AutoCAD command.

Digitizer Input: Controls the type of digitizer used to control AutoCAD.

Keystrokes: Determines whether the AutoCAD Classic (standard keystrokes) or the Menu File (accelerator keystrokes) is used. Accelerator keys are key sequences programmed through customization of the AutoCAD menu.

Font: The Font button displays a dialog box that allows you to pick the font AutoCAD uses for text display in the graphics or text windows.

Color: The Color button displays a dialog box used to Specify the colors of elements in the AutoCAD application window.

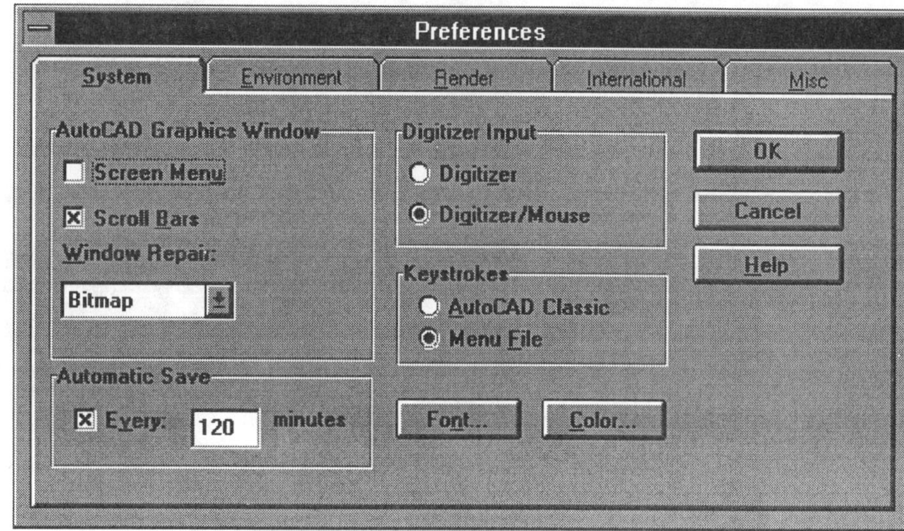

Figure 1.4
Preferences - Systems dialog box

ENVIRONMENT (Refer to Figure 1.5)

Directories: This area controls where AutoCAD looks for program elements.

Files: This specifies the location of the help, alternate menu, and log files. The log file box controls whether the text displayed in the text window is also written to a log file.

Memory: Controls the amount of memory used by AutoCAD to write the drawing file during screen operations.

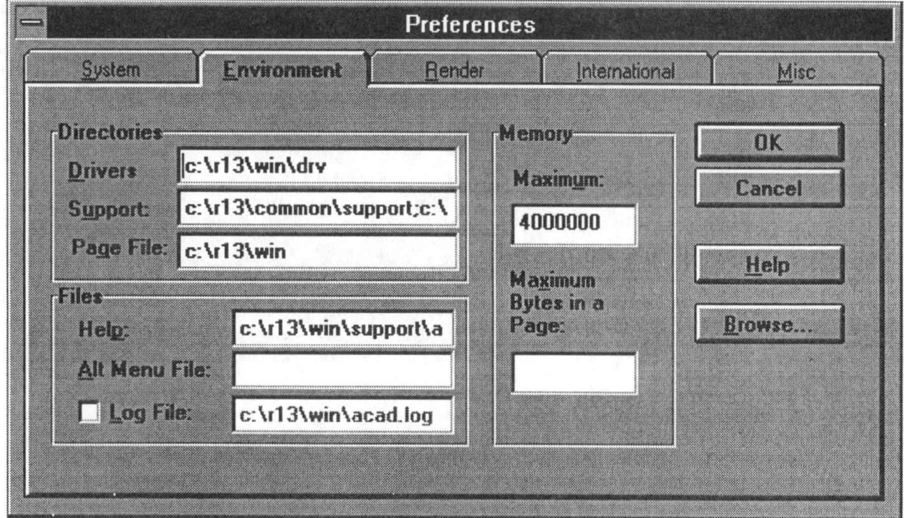

Figure 1.5
Preferences - Environment dialog box

RENDER (Refer to Figure 1.6)
This folder controls the location of files for the rendering environment.

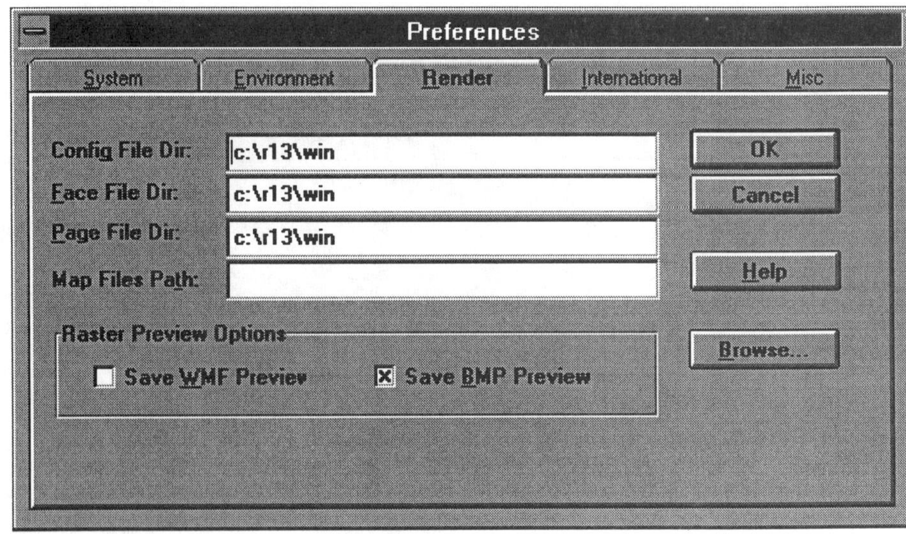

Figure 1.6
Preferences - Render dialog box

INTERNATIONAL (Refer to Figure 1.7)
International Settings: Specifies whether English or metric units of measurement are used.
Prototype Drawing: Specifies the type of prototype drawing to be used.

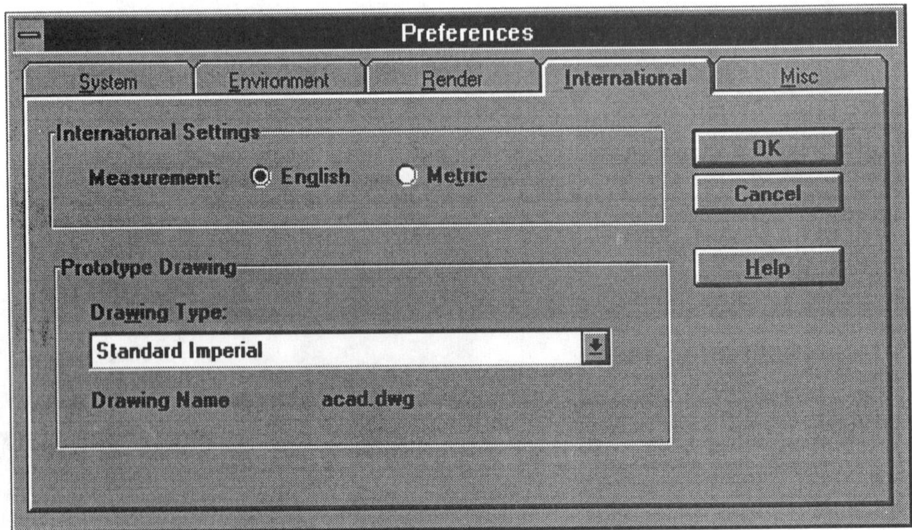

Figure 1.7
Preferences - International dialog box

MISC (Refer to Figure 1.8)
Options: This area allows you to specify the text editor and font

mapping file used by the MTEXT command. It also
controls the size of the AutoCAD application window and
drawing view upon startup.

Text Window: Specifies the number of lines used for the history
area of the command window and the number of lines
visible when the command window is docked.

Plot Spooling: Specifies the conditions used when plot spooling
(plotting in the background).

Figure 1.8
Preferences - Misc dialog box

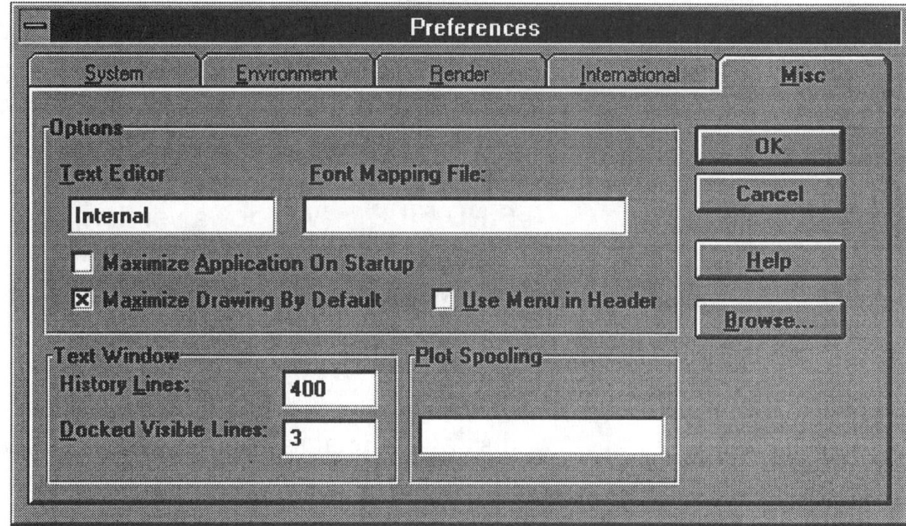

1.6 Opening a Drawing

This section will introduce you to the new drawing viewing options
when you want to open an existing drawing. These options are available
in the DOS or Windows versions of AutoCAD R13. Refer to Figure 1.9
for an illustration of the Select File dialog box for the Windows version.

Figure 1.9
OPEN/Select File dialog box

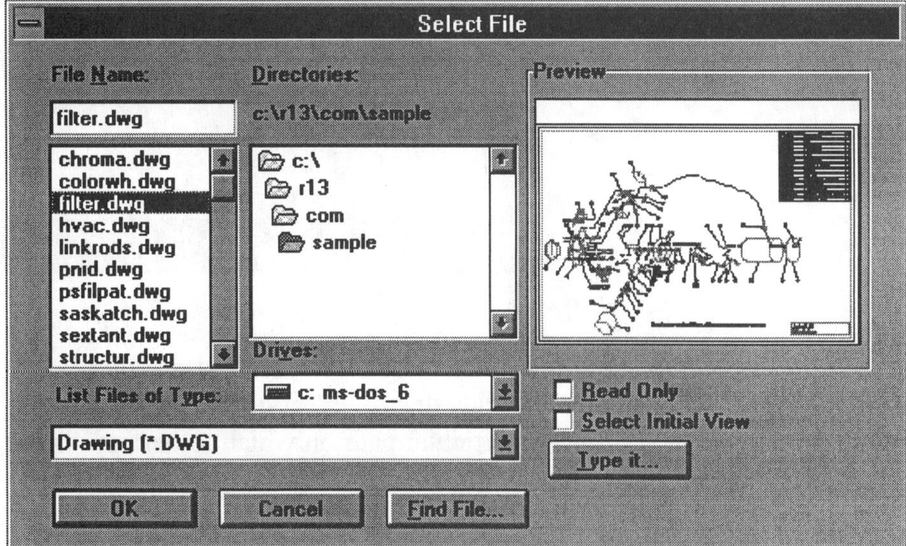

PREVIEW

A preview window has been added to the Select File dialog box. Refer to Figure 1.9. When you highlight a drawing from the file list a bitmap image of the drawing will be displayed in the preview box. When a drawing is saved in R13 a bitmap image of the current view is saved in the file as well. You may notice that the size of R13 drawings is larger than R12. This is one reason. However, the preview feature can be a quick way of identifying drawings. You can also add bitmap images to drawing files previous to R13 by using the MAKEPREVIEW command. MAKEPREVIEW creates a compressed .bmp file of the current view and places the file in the same directory as the drawing file. If this .bmp file and .dwg file reside in the same directory when you use the OPEN command, the Select File dialog box will display the image in the Preview box.

FIND FILE   (Windows version)

There has been a new button added to the Select File dialog box called Find File. When you pick this button, a Browse/Search dialog box is displayed. Refer to Figure 1.10.

The Browse filefolder displays small bitmap images for R13 drawing files in the selected subdirectory. You can sort by file type and display the images at three different sizes: small, medium, and large. To open one of the displayed files, click on the desired image. Refer to Figure 1.10.

Figure 1.10
Browse filefolder

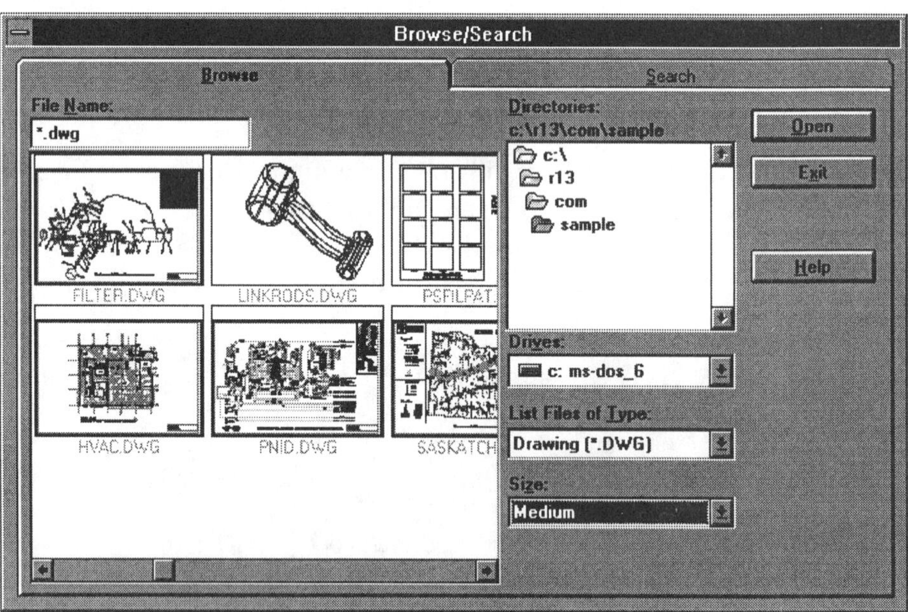

The Search filefolder allows you to specify a search pattern to help locate drawings. You can specify a file type and date filter, as well as the particular path on which to perform the search. Refer to Figure 1.11.

Figure 1.11
Search filefolder

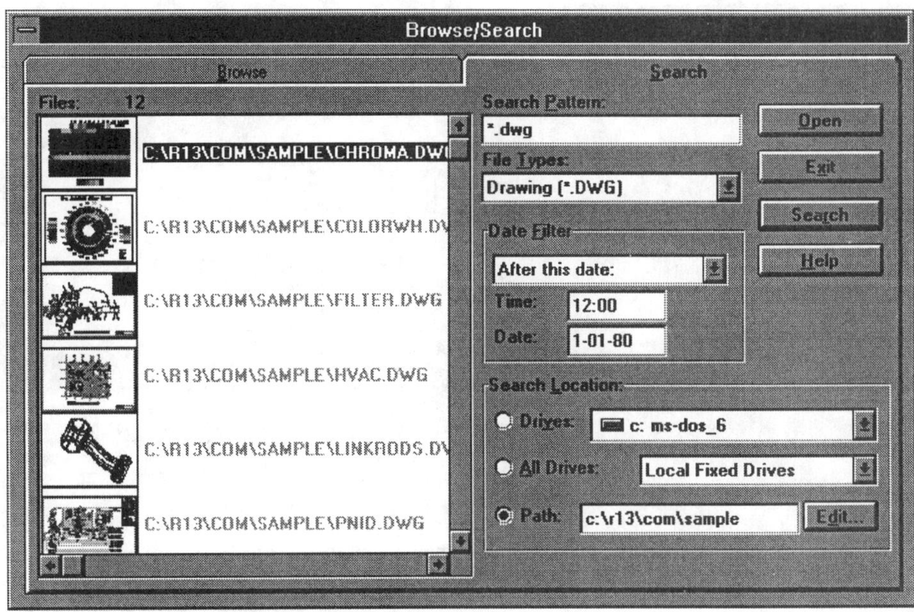

1.7 Saving Files

Always save drawings frequently, especially when using a new version of a program. When you use the SAVEAS or SAVE command, your file will be saved in the R13 drawing file format. When it is in this format, you will not be able to recall the drawing using the R12 version of AutoCAD. If you know ahead of time that you might need to do this, use the SAVEASR12 command. This command saves the drawing file in the R12 format, stripping away any of the R13 advanced features. Remember that, since you are going to an earlier version, it is possible that some of the new entities may not transfer properly. So be prepared.

1.8 Importing and Export

The importing and exporting of files in R13 has now been grouped to make it easier to access. In the DOS and Windows versions they are grouped under the File menu. In the Windows version, dialog boxes are used to facilitate the selection of the available file types. Figures 1.12 and 1.13 show the two dialog boxes. The pop-up lists for file types have been expanded so that you can see the various file types that can be imported and exported. 3D Studio's 3DS format can now be imported and exported directly.

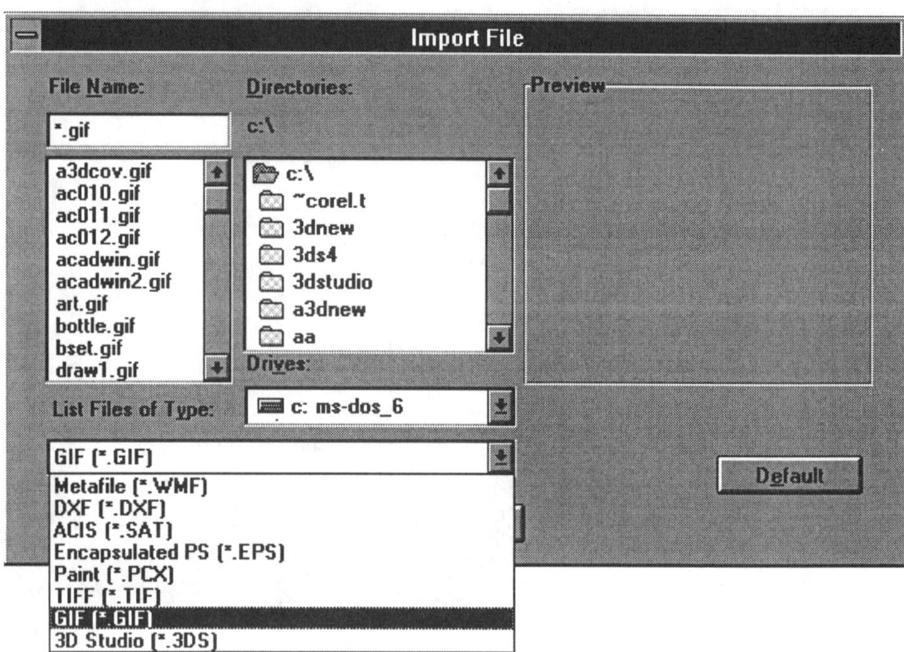

Figure 1.12
Import File dialog box

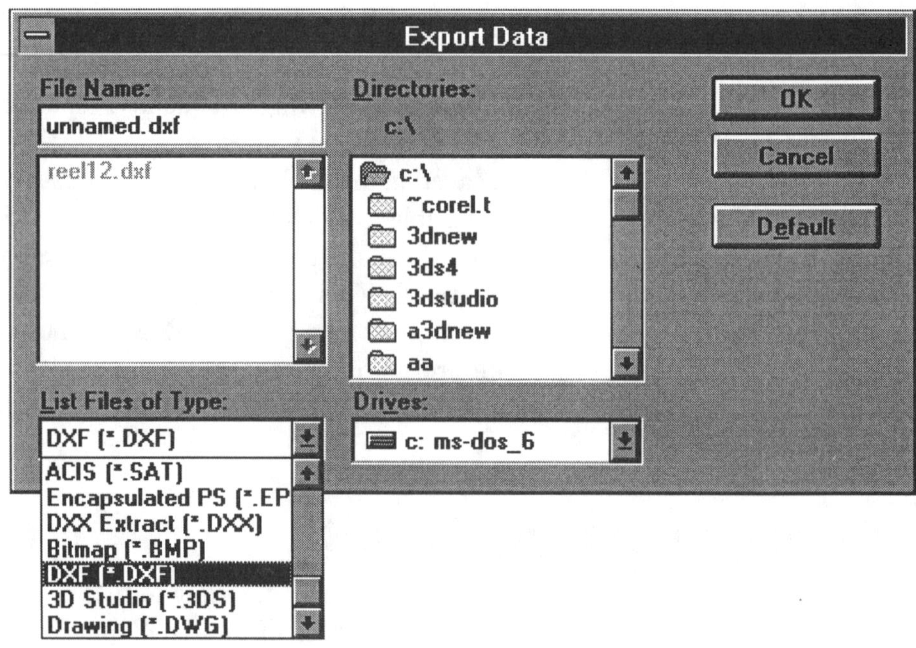

Figure 1.13
Export Data dialog box

1.9 Highlights

The following are some highlights of the changes from release 12 to 13.

- The dimension commands have been streamlined such that they can be

entered directly from the command line.
- The new dimension style format and set-up procedure is more visually oriented.
- Annotation has been enhanced with the addition of multi-line text that is treated as a single paragraph and a built-in spell checker.
- Hatching as been made associative to allow editing of the hatch and its boundaries.
- There has been an addition of new objects such as true ellipse, multi-line, and construction geometry.
- There are enhancements to existing commands such as EXTEND, TRIM, and FILLET
- Additional Object Snap modes such as apparent intersection and relative point have been added.

CHAPTER 2

Drawing Aids and Viewing

2.1 Introduction

The chapter will document the changes to the drawing aids and viewing commands and the addition of new commands under those categories. As well, the Standard and Object Properties toolbars are explained. The icons included come from the Windows release 13 version.

2.2 Standard Toolbar (Windows version)

The Standard toolbar is used to access the common Windows commands such as new, open, and save, as well as to easily access object snap and other AutoCAD drawing aids. The different icons of the toolbar are identified in Figure 2.1.

Figure 2.1
Standard toolbar

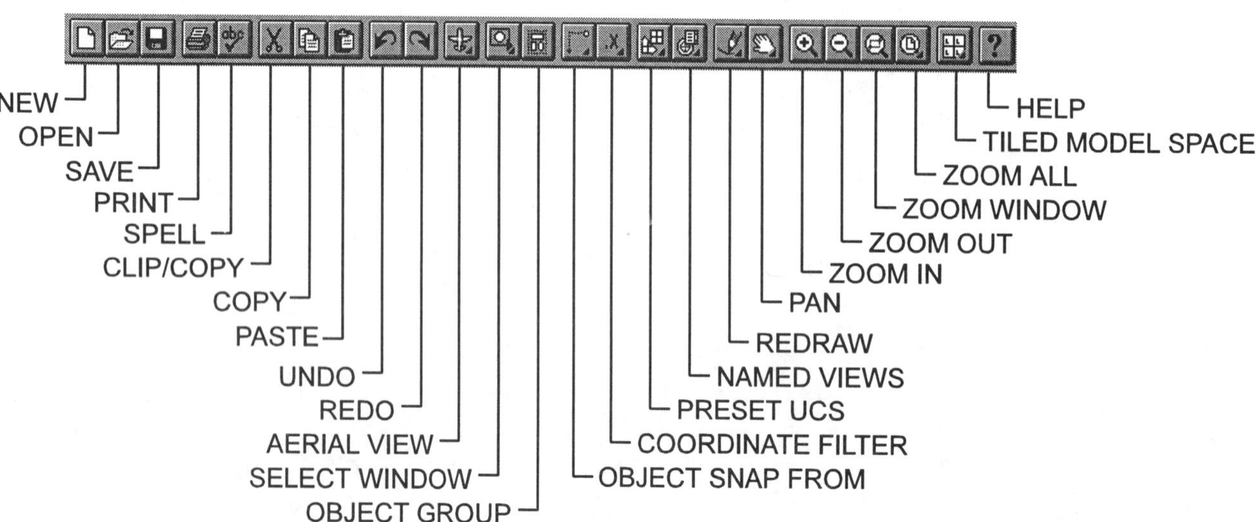

Be sure to notice the small black triangles in the lower right corner of some of the tools. This indicates that there is a flyout that contains additional tool icons. For instance, the Aerial View tool contains the tools for opening the various toolbars. The following are the flyouts for the various tools on the Standard toolbar along with descriptions of the tools contained within.

Aerial View flyout

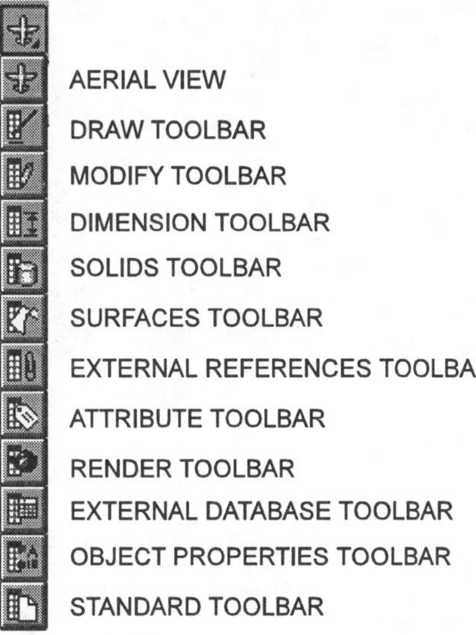

AERIAL VIEW

DRAW TOOLBAR

MODIFY TOOLBAR

DIMENSION TOOLBAR

SOLIDS TOOLBAR

SURFACES TOOLBAR

EXTERNAL REFERENCES TOOLBAR

ATTRIBUTE TOOLBAR

RENDER TOOLBAR

EXTERNAL DATABASE TOOLBAR

OBJECT PROPERTIES TOOLBAR

STANDARD TOOLBAR

Select Window Flyout

SELECT WINDOW

SELECT CROSSING

SELECT GROUP

SELECT PREVIOUS

SELECT LAST

SELECT ALL

SELECT WINDOW POLYGON

SELECT CROSSING POLYGON

SELECT FENCE

SELECT ADD

SELECT REMOVE

SELECTION FILTERS

Object Snap From flyout

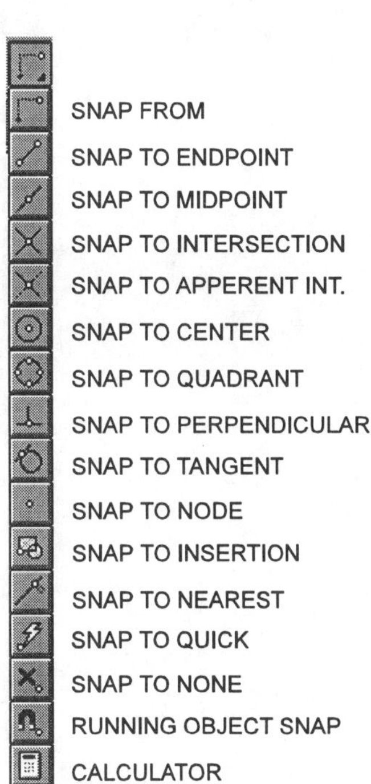

SNAP FROM

SNAP TO ENDPOINT

SNAP TO MIDPOINT

SNAP TO INTERSECTION

SNAP TO APPERENT INT.

SNAP TO CENTER

SNAP TO QUADRANT

SNAP TO PERPENDICULAR

SNAP TO TANGENT

SNAP TO NODE

SNAP TO INSERTION

SNAP TO NEAREST

SNAP TO QUICK

SNAP TO NONE

RUNNING OBJECT SNAP

CALCULATOR

Coordinate Filter flyout

.X COORDINATE FILTER

.Y COORDINATE FILTER

.Z COORDINATE FILTER

.XY COORDINATE FILTER

.XZ COORDINATE FILTER

.YZ COORDINATE FILTER

Preset UCS flyout

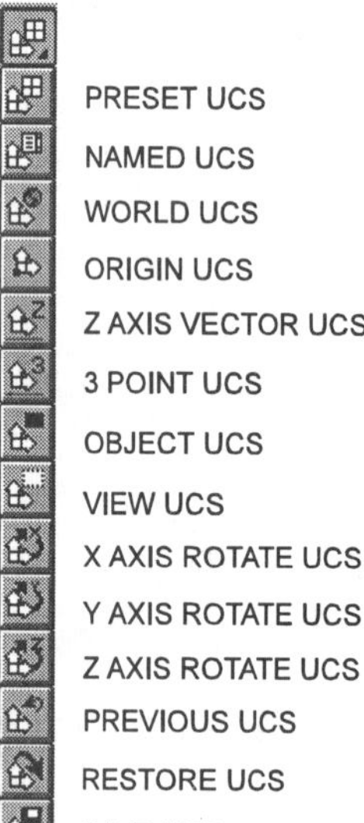

PRESET UCS
NAMED UCS
WORLD UCS
ORIGIN UCS
Z AXIS VECTOR UCS
3 POINT UCS
OBJECT UCS
VIEW UCS
X AXIS ROTATE UCS
Y AXIS ROTATE UCS
Z AXIS ROTATE UCS
PREVIOUS UCS
RESTORE UCS
SAVE UCS

Named Views flyout

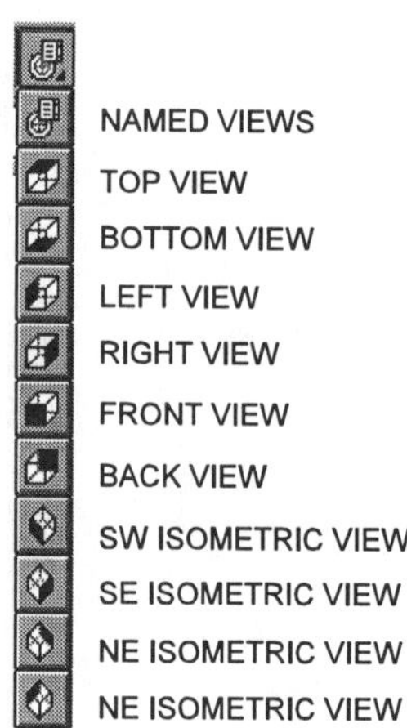

NAMED VIEWS
TOP VIEW
BOTTOM VIEW
LEFT VIEW
RIGHT VIEW
FRONT VIEW
BACK VIEW
SW ISOMETRIC VIEW
SE ISOMETRIC VIEW
NE ISOMETRIC VIEW
NE ISOMETRIC VIEW

Redraw flyout

REDRAW
REDRAW ALL

Zoom All flyout

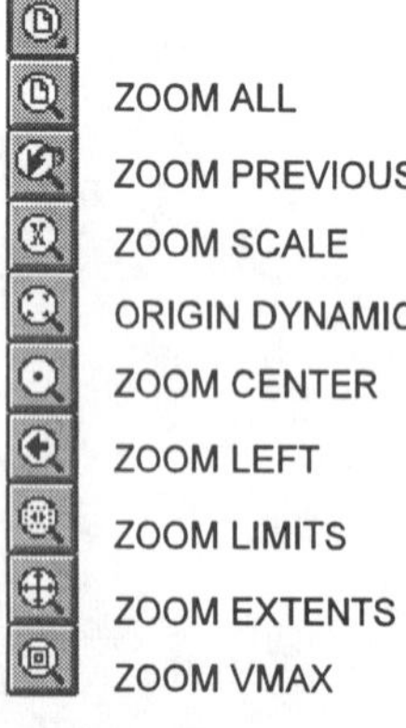

ZOOM ALL
ZOOM PREVIOUS
ZOOM SCALE
ORIGIN DYNAMIC
ZOOM CENTER
ZOOM LEFT
ZOOM LIMITS
ZOOM EXTENTS
ZOOM VMAX

Pan flyout

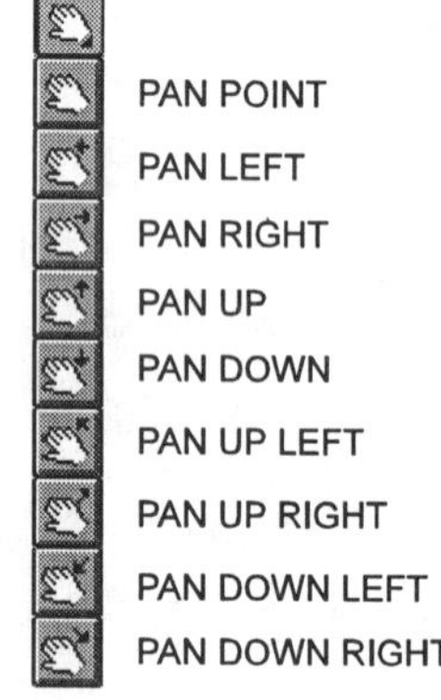

PAN POINT
PAN LEFT
PAN RIGHT
PAN UP
PAN DOWN
PAN UP LEFT
PAN UP RIGHT
PAN DOWN LEFT
PAN DOWN RIGHT

Tiled Model Space flyout

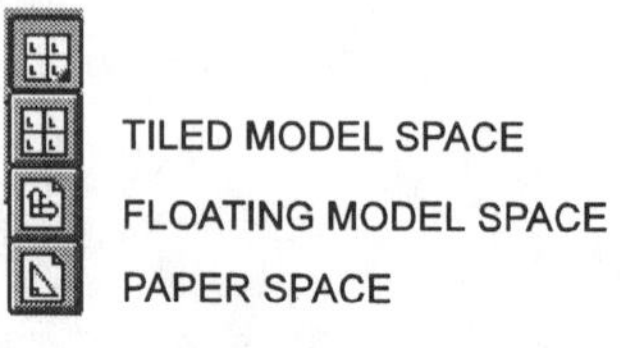

TILED MODEL SPACE
FLOATING MODEL SPACE
PAPER SPACE

 # Object Snap

There are now two additional object snap modes - Apparent Intersection and From.

Command line equivalent: APPINT or APP
Apparent Intersection snaps to where two objects would intersect, even if their geometry does not actually intersect. Refer to Figure 2 . 2 .

Command: **Circle**
3P/2P/TTRr/<center point>: **APP**
of   **pick one line**
and   **pick other line**   (apparent intersection is calculated)
Diameter/ <Radius><0>: **enter value as usual**

Figure 2.2
Apparent Intersection object snap

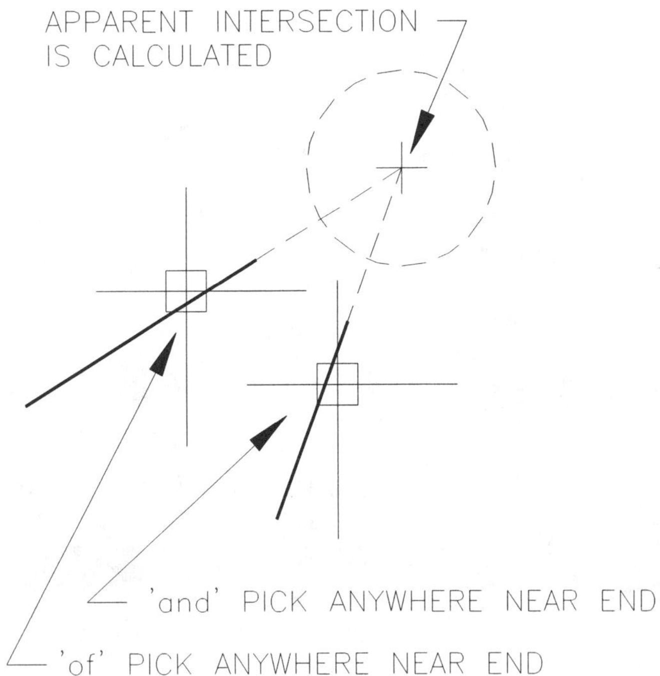

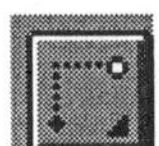

Command line equivalent: FROM
From object snap is used to establish a temporary reference point for use with relative offsets. For instance, if you wanted to draw a circle a specific distance from a known point, you would use the From object snap to establish the known point and then enter the relative distance to the center of the new circle. Refer to Figure 2.3.

Command: **Circle**
3P/2P/TTRr/<center point>: **FROM**
Basepoint: **endpoint**   (enter object snap to assist)
of   **pick 'from' basepoint**
<offset>: **@4,-2**
Diameter/ <Radius><0>: **enter value as usual**

Figure 2.3
From object snap

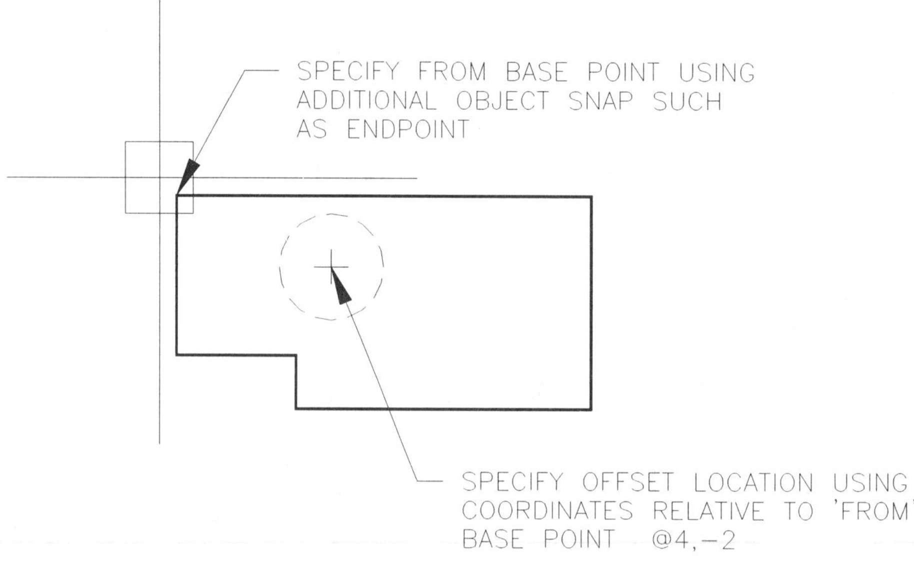

2.4 **Object Properties Toolbar** (Windows version)

The Object Properties toolbar is used to access the various object property
features such as layer and linetype. Refer to Figure 2.4.

Figure 2.4
Object Properties toolbar

The toolbar is separated into several sections:

Layers tool
Displays the Layers Control dialog box.

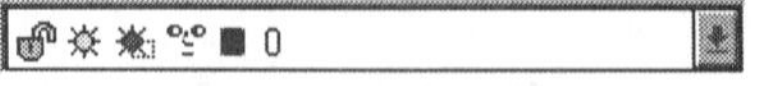

Layer Control pop-up list tool
Quick access to some of the more commonly used layer options such as:
locking, freezing, VPfreeze, ON/OFF, and setting the current layer. These
are set by picking on the appropriate small icon.

Color Control tool

Shows the condition of the current color. If it shows the layer icon then color is set to Bylayer. If it is a solid color, then the color is overriding the current layer color. Picking on the tool allows you to set the status of the current color.

Linetype tool
Displays the Select Linetype dialog box. It is used to load linetypes as well as to set the current linetype status.

Linetype Control pop-up list tool
Allows quick access to a list of the currently loaded linetypes and lets you choose from them to override the linetype for the current layer.

Object Creation tool
Displays the Object Creation Modes dialog box.

Multiline Style tool
Displays the Multiline Styles dialog box used to set the current multiline style and to create and modify others.

Properties tool
Accesses the DDMODIFY command used to modify the properties of individual objects.

List tool
Accesses the LIST command used to display the properties of objects without modifying them.

2.5 Aerial View

The Aerial View feature is useful for both moving about the drawing (pan) and magnifying certain areas (zoom). This feature is available in both the DOS and Windows versions, though the DOS version does not have all the features of the Windows version. Refer to Figure 2.5 for an illustration of the Windows version.

    To invoke the Aerial View in Windows, pick the icon or enter DSVIEWER on the command line. In the DOS version you enter AV on the command line. It is not available in paper space in either version and your system must be configured for Windows' accelerated display driver with the Display List option. The following are the Windows version options:

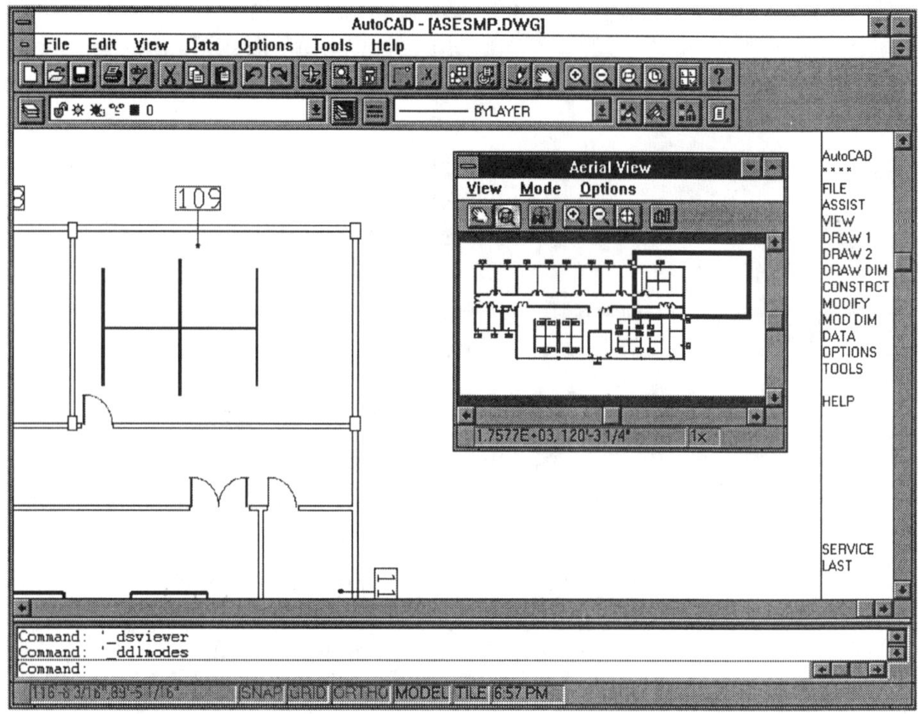

AERIAL VIEW

View Menu: This menu is used to zoom in, zoom out, and globally zoom (displays entire drawing) the drawing shown in the Aerial View window. This can also be accomplished by using the tools at the top of the window as shown here.

 Zoom In tool

 Zoom Out tool

 Zoom Global tool

Mode Menu: This menu is used to switch between Zoom and Pan modes. In the Zoom mode, use the cursor to specify the area to zoom in or out on. In Pan mode, use the cursor to point to the area you want displayed on the screen. This can also be accomplished using the following tools:

 Zoom mode tool

 Pan mode tool

Options Menu: This menu is used to set the following options:

Auto Viewport: When active, this option displays the model space view of the active viewport.

Dynamic Update: When active, this option causes the view to be updated whenever you modify the drawing.

Locator Magnification: This option is used to control the amount of magnification (up to 32 times) used with the locator tool.

Display Statistics: This option displays how much memory is being used by the display list driver.

Locator Tool: This tool is used to specify an area on the drawing to be displayed in the Aerial View. When you pick this tool and hold the pick button down, the cursor becomes a circle with cross-hairs. You move this locator symbol onto the drawing to specify the areas to be shown in the Aerial View window and on the display.

CHAPTER 3

Draw

3.1 Introduction

This chapter deals with the changes to the existing draw commands and the new draw commands to create new objects types. Some previous draw commands have been replaced with more advanced ones of similar types.

Object creation commands for text, dimensions, and solid modeling will be explained in later chapters.

3.2 Old and New

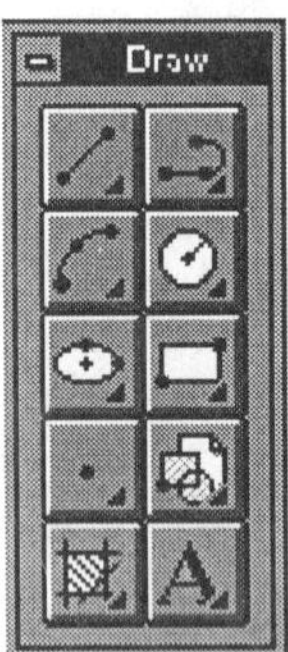

The following are the highlights of the changes to the draw commands. These will be explained in detail in their own sections.

There have been enhancements made to the BHATCH and ELLIPSE commands. The BHATCH command now creates associative hatching and the ELLIPSE command now creates a new object type - a true ellipse. In the past the ELLIPSE command created an approximate ellipse using polylines.

The BPOLY command has been replaced by the more functional BOUNDARY command which creates regions or polyline boundaries. Regions have been added as integral objects in AutoCAD. These will be explained further in the chapter on solid modeling.

The DLINE command has been replaced by the MLINE command. The DLINE command was used to create double line entities. The MLINE command creates a new object type - MLINE.

Another new object type and command have been added - the SPLINE. This new object gives you more control over the previous spline object. Previously you had to modify a polyline to create an approximate spline.

To aid in construction, two new objects have been added - XLINE and RAY. XLINE creates construction lines that stretch into infinity while RAY creates a line object that stretches from a specific point to infinity.

3.3 Linetype Scale

One major change that relates to the creation of all objects, old or new, is the addition of the individual linetype scale property for all objects. This property works in addition to the global LTSCALE. Now you can select individual objects and modify their linetype scale factor. It works by multiplying an individual linetype scale value by the global linetype scale value to arrive at an individual object linetype scale. For instance, if you set the global LTSCALE to 5 and then modified an individual object's linetype scale factor to 2, the linetype scale for that object would be: 5 x 2 = 10. Figure 3.1 depicts the Object Creation Modes dialog box, showing the addition of the Linetype Scale factor box.

Figure 3.1
Object Creation Modes dialog box

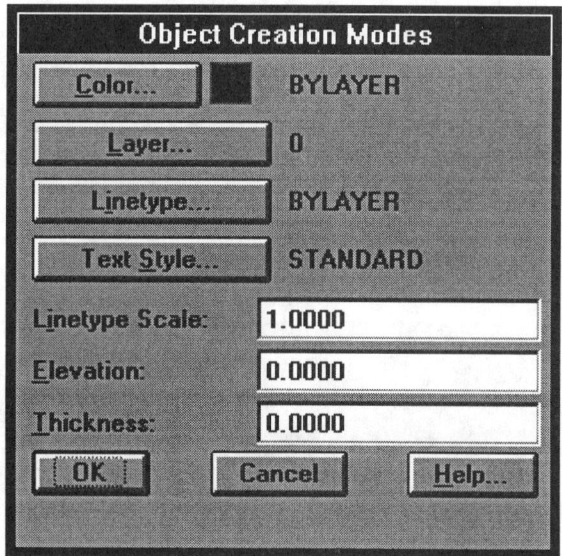

3.4 Hatching

The Boundary Hatch dialog box has undergone a rearrangement. Refer to Figure 3.2. Instead of picking hatch icons from an array, you either pick on a single icon screen to cycle through the different hatch patterns or pick from a pop-up list beside the Pattern heading.

The new BHATCH command now uses automatic island detection to internal objects within the hatch boundary. This is controlled from the

Advanced Options dialog box. Refer to Figure 3.3. If you check the Retain Boundaries box, you can specify the Object Type to be either a polyline or a region.

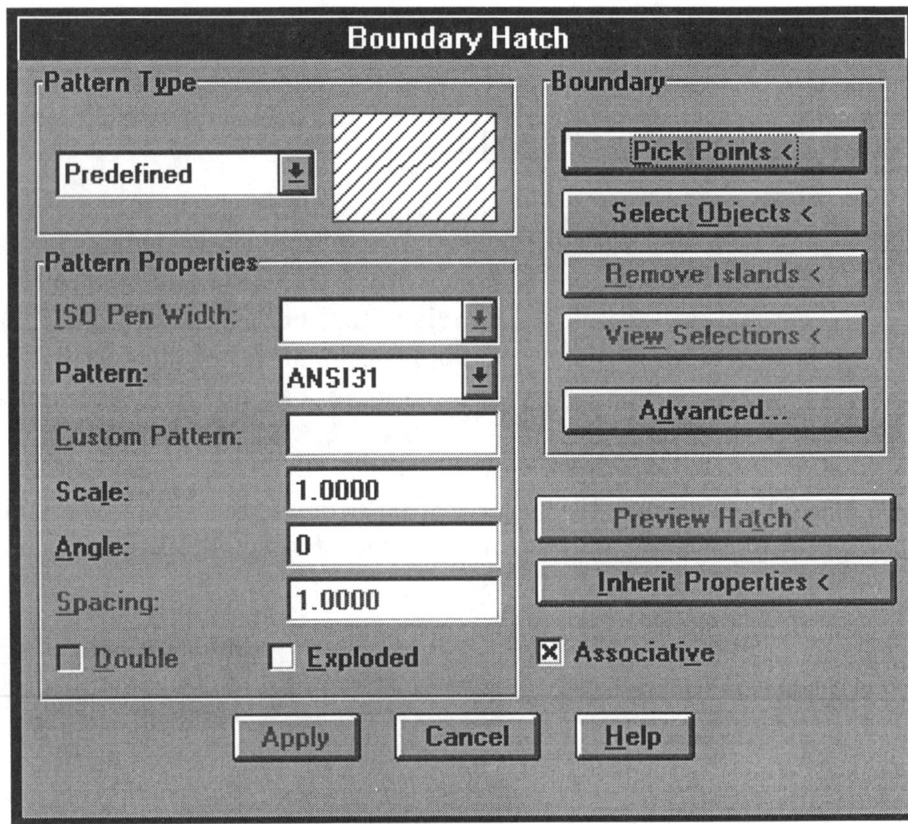

Figure 3.2
Boundary Hatch dialog box

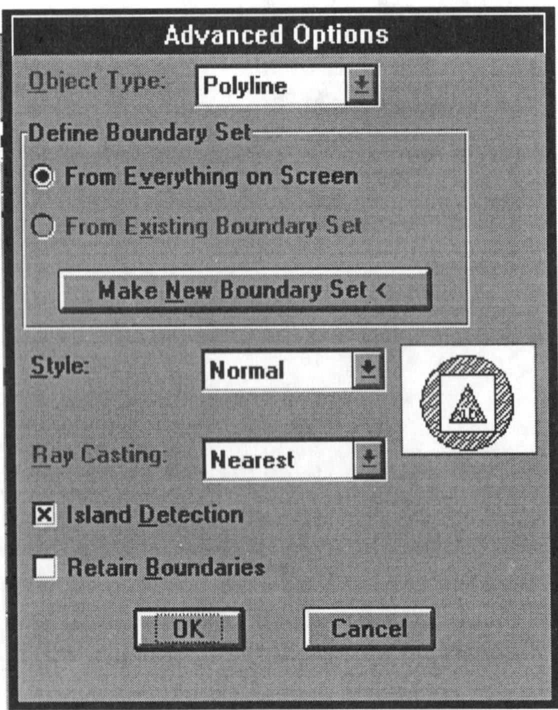

Figure 3.3
Advanced Options of the Boundary Hatch dialog box

The second enhancement is the addition of associative hatching. Observe the Associative check box in the lower corner of the Boundary Hatch dialog box in Figure 3.2. When this is checked, any new hatch that is created retains its hatch properties, such as boundary and pattern. When you edit the boundary objects used to create the hatch, the hatch will change automatically. This is something you will have to be careful about. Changing hatch boundary objects can have some strange results. The benefit of associative hatch is that you can edit the hatch later on using the new HATCHEDIT command. This command presents you with a dialog box similar the Boundary Hatch dialog box, allowing you change the hatch pattern, scale, and other properties.

BOUNDARY Command

The BOUNDARY command is really an extension of the BHATCH command. Instead of adding hatches to your drawing, the BOUNDARY command simply creates the boundary as an object. Refer to Figure 3.4. This command replaces the BPOLY command, mainly because you can now create boundaries made of the new region objects as well as polylines. The Boolean Subtract Islands option is used to automatically delete island objects that might lie within an outer-boundary from the calculated boundary. For instance, if you wanted to make a boundary of a room, but the room contained furniture, the furniture would simply be removed from the calculated boundary. The BOUNDARY tool can be found under the Rectangle tool flyout.

Figure 3.4
Boundary Creation dialog box

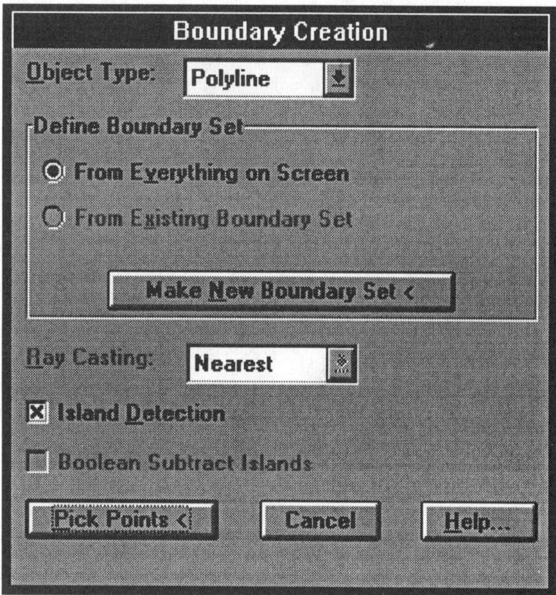

3.5 Ellipse

There has be no major change to the standard functionality of the ELLIPSE command. You create an ellipse just as you did in the past. The change lies in the object type created.

The new ELLIPSE command can now create true ellipical objects. When you create an ellipse with this method, you can test this by listing its properties. It will be listed as an ellipse object. If you desire to create an ellipse using the past polyline method, you can still do it by changing the PELLIPSE system variable. If the variable is set to 0, then true ellipse objects are created. If you set the variable to 1, then polyline representations of an ellipse are created.

One additional feature has been added to the ellipse command, and that is the ability to draw elliptical arcs. By selecting the appropriate icon or selecting the Arc option of the ellipse command, you first specify the parameters of the ellipse and then specify the arc length by start and ending angles. Refer to Figure 3.5 for an illustration of an ellipse and ellipse arc.

True Ellipse objects cannot be exploded. If you think you might what to break an ellipse into several pieces, use a polyline ellipse instead.

Figure 3.5
Ellipse and Ellipse arc

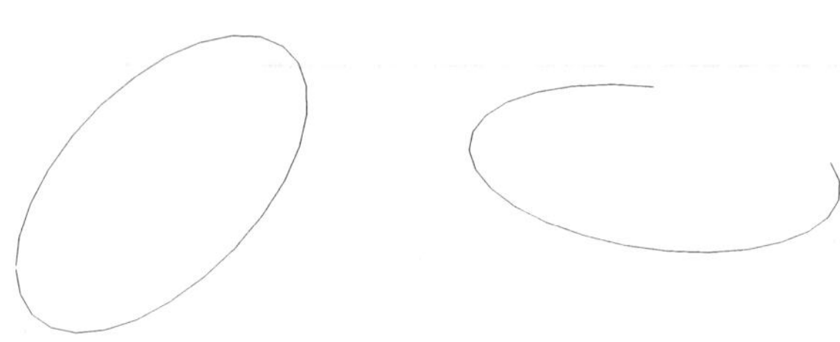

3.6 Multilines

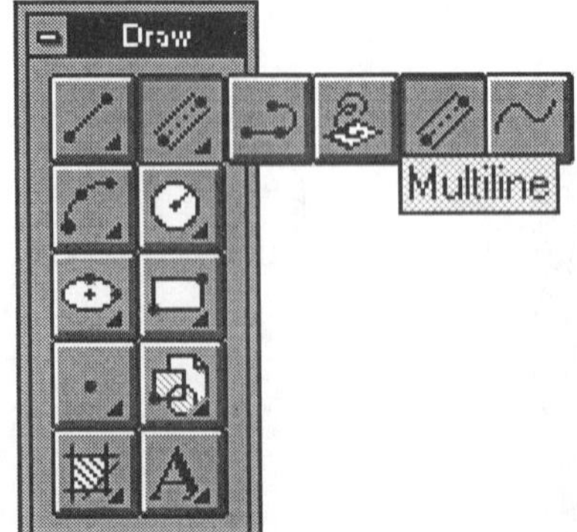

The MLINE command gives you the ability to draw multiple parallel lines by simply specifying a start and end point. The Multiline tool can be found under the Polyline tool flyout. The lines can be any distance apart, different linetypes, and closed at either or both ends. This new command and new object replace the previous DLINE command that drew only two parallel line objects. Figure 3.6 shows some city streets drawn with MLINE and identifies some of the terminology associated with the MLINE options.

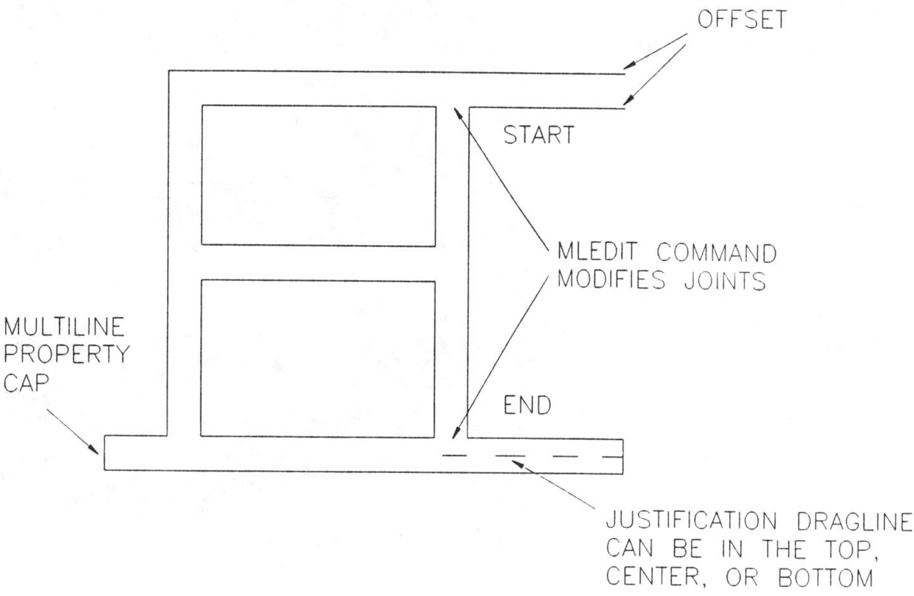

Figure 3.6
Using the MLINE command

Command: **MLINE**
Justification = Top, Scale = 1.00, Style = STANDARD
Justification/Scale/STyle/ <From point>

The following is an explanation of the various options presented to you.

Justification — This is used to locate the multiple lines in reference to the pick point. An imaginary line called the dragline is drawn from the start pick point and the end pick point. You can decide whether this line will be in the center (zero), at the top, or at the bottom.

Scale — This is a scale factor applied to the distance between the parallel lines. The initial distance is set when you create the multiline style (MLSTYLE).

Style — This option allows you to choose the style of multiline created previously.

Multiline Styles

The MLSTYLE command displays the dialog box shown in Figure 3.7. This box is used to set the current multiline style, create new multiline styles, and modify existing ones. The following text provides a description of the dialog box areas.

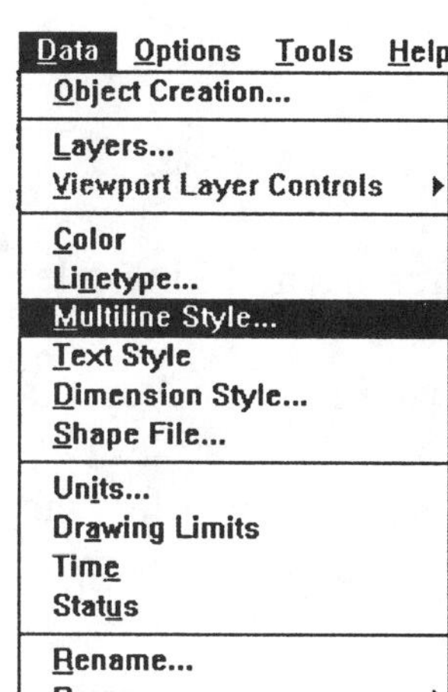

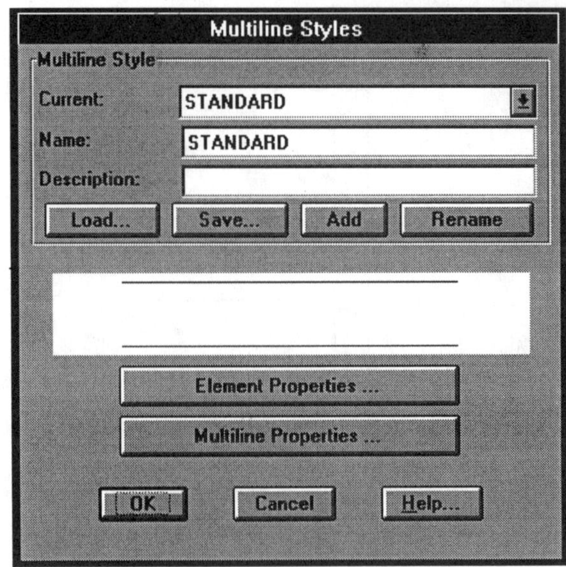

Current	Displays the name of the current multiline style from a pop-up list.
Name	Creates a new multiline from a previous multiline.
Description	Adds extra information to describe the multiline's purpose, such as "interior wall".
Load	Loads multiline styles from existing files that have the extension .MLN.
Save	Saves multiline styles to an MLN file.
Add	Allows you to add a multiline style.
Rename	Allows you to change the name of a multiline style.
Icon Box	Displays the appearance of the current multilinestyle.
Element Properties	Displays a dialog box as shown in Figure 3.8. It is used to create and modify multiline styles. By adding and deleting lines, changing their color, and linetype, you can create a complex line style.
Multiline Properties	Displays the dialog box shown in Figure 3.9. It is used to further modify the multiline properties by adding various caps on the start and end of the multiline and filling in a multiline with a solid color.

Figure 3.8
Element Properties dialog box

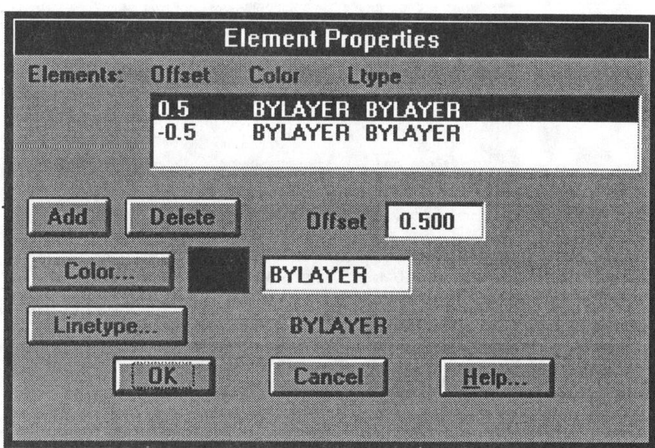

Figure 3.9
Multiline Properties dialog box

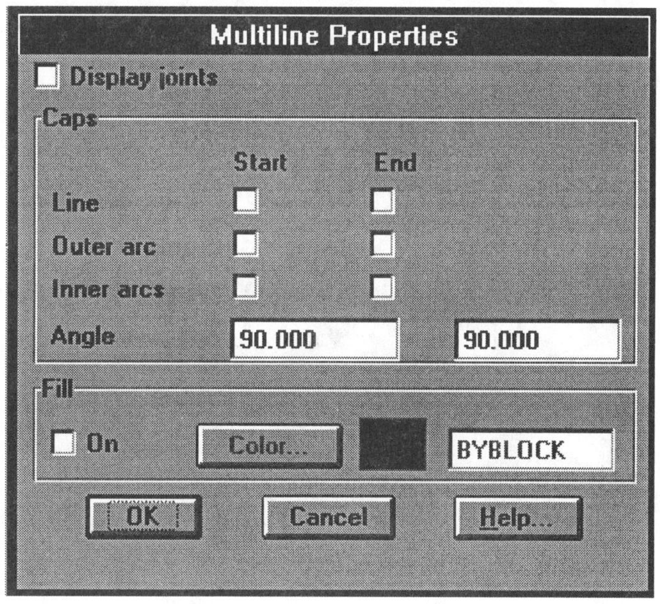

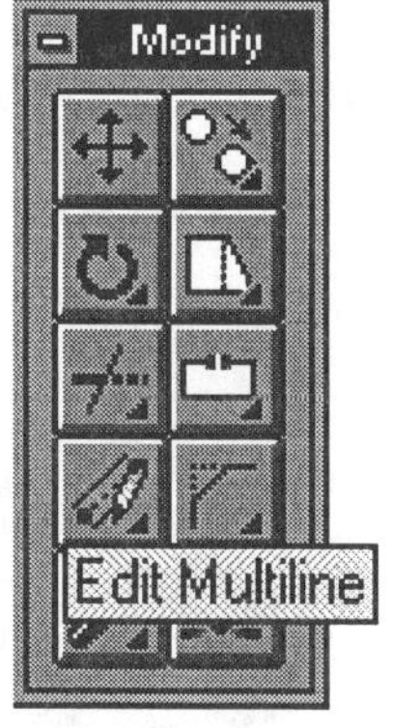

Multiline Editing

Since multilines are a different object type than regular lines, you must edit them using special tools. The tools are used to join multilines together in a variety of joint types.

The MLEDIT command is used to edit a multiline by displaying a dialog box like the one shown in Figure 3.10. To use the display tools, pick the icon representing the desired editing command. When the icon is picked, a description of the modification is displayed at the bottom of the dialog box.

Figure 3.10
Multiline Edit Tools dialog box

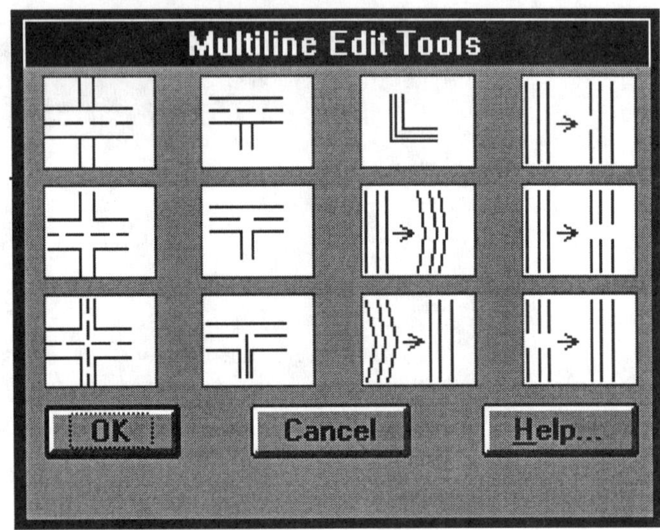

The following demonstrates the use of the MLEDIT command. Refer to Figure 3.11 for an illustration of the visual product.

Command: **MLEDIT**
You are presented with the dialog box as shown in Figure 3.10. **Pick** the appropriate tool from the dialog box. In this case it is the Open Tee tool.

Select first Mline: **pick** the intersecting Mline
Select second Mline: **pick** the Mline to open.
The second mline is then modified and the first mline is joined to it.

Figure 3.11
Using MLEDIT command

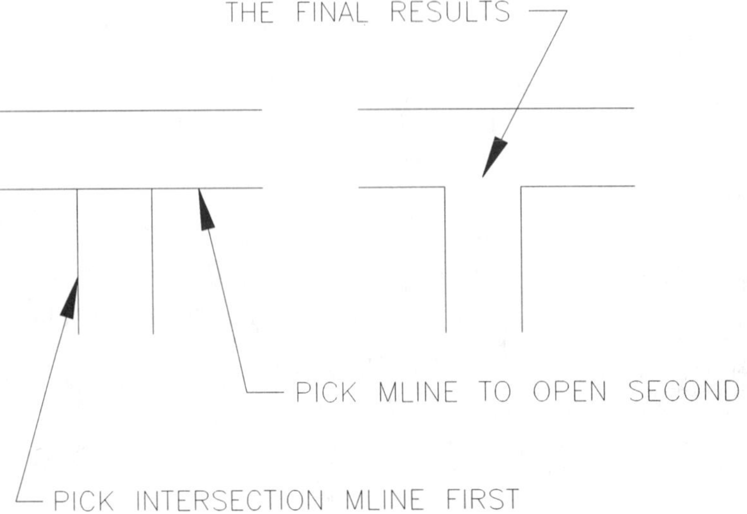

32

3.7 Spline

The SPLINE command creates a quadratic or cubic spline curve that is referred to as a free-form, non-uniform, rational B-spline (NURBS). It produces more accurate curves that the regularly edited polylines, and it also uses less file space than a multisegmented polyline. A spline is created by specifying control points through which the curve passes. The Spline tool is found under the Polyline flyout in the Draw toolbar. Refer to Figure 3.12 and the following command definition.

Command: **SPLINE**
Object <Enter first point>: **enter start point (P1)**
Enter point: **enter the second point along the spline (P2)**
Close/Fit Tolerance/<Enter point>: **continue to enter points (P3,P4) and then press <Enter>**
Enter start tangent: **enter a point that an imaginary line passes through from the spline (P5)** (This bends the start of the spline so that it forms a tangent point with the imaginary line.)
Enter end tangent: **enter a point that an imaginary line passes through from the spline (P6)** (This bends the end of the spline so that it forms a tangent point with the imaginary line.)

Figure 3.12
Using the SPLINE command

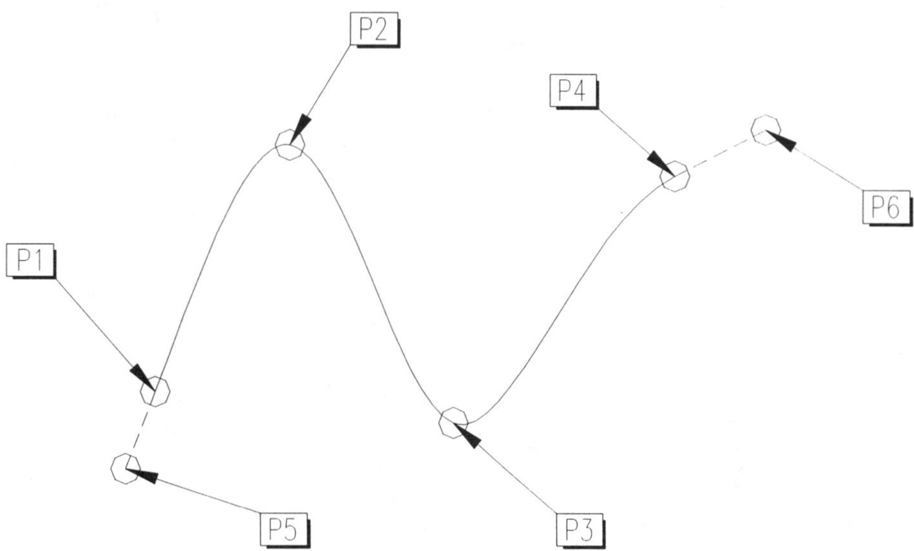

The following is an explanation of the Close and Fit Tolerance options of the SPLINE command:

Object   Converts 2D or 3D spline-fit polylines into splines.

Close   Closes the spline so that it has no start or end.

Fit Tolerance   Normally this is set to 0, which forces the spline to be drawn through the control points. However, you can give a tolerance value that allows the spline to "stray" from the control point up to the given tolerance value.

Editing Splines

The SPLINEDIT command is used to edit splines. You will find the SPLINEEDIT tool under the Edit Polyline tool flyout in the Modify toolbar. Its command definition follows:

Command: **SPLINEDIT**
Select Spline:
Fit Data/Close/Move Vertex/Refine/ rEverese/Undo/eXit <X>:

Its options include the following:

Fit Data   Allows you to add and modify points and alter the tolerance.

Close   Closes an open spline. This is replaced with Open if you selected a closed spline.

Move Vertex   Allows you to move a control point.

Refine   Adds control points to a spline automatically, up to 26.

rEverse   Reverses the start and finish points of the spline.

Undo   Undoes any modifications to the selected spline.

3.8 Construction Lines

The new XLINE command creates an infinite line. The purpose of this object is to create construction lines that extend across your drawing no matter the size of the drawing. These lines can be used to assist in the construction or placement of other geometry. The XLINE tool can be found under the LINE tool flyout. Refer to Figure 3.13 and the following command description.

Command: **XLINE**
Hor/Ver/Ang/Bisect/Offset/<From point>: **specify a point or option**

Hor   Creates a horizontal xline passing through a selected point.

Ver   Creates a vertical xline passing through a selected point.

Ang   Creates an xline at a specified angle.

Bisect   Creates an xline that passes through the selected angle vertex and bisects the angle between the first and second line.

Offset   Creates an xline parallel to another object.

From point Specifies the location (P1) of the infinite xline and the point through which it will pass. The Through option prompts you for the second point (P2) that xline will pass through.

Figure 3.13
Using the XLINE command

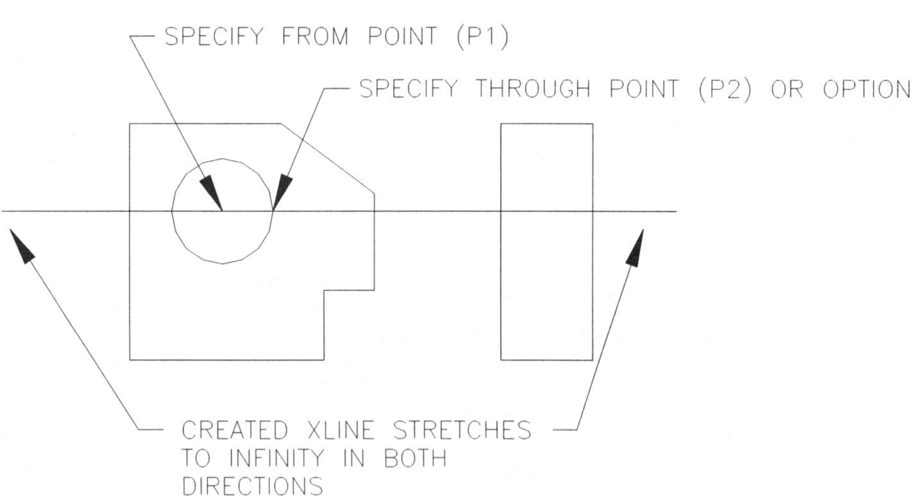

 Rays

The new RAY command creates a semi-infinite line. Like the xlines these lines are used for drawing construction purposes. Rays only extend to infinity in one direction, extending from a specified start point. To use the RAY command, you need to specify the start point (P1) and then the point through which the ray will pass (P2). The RAY tool can be found under the LINE tool flyout. Refer to Figure 3.14.

Figure 3.14
Using the RAY command

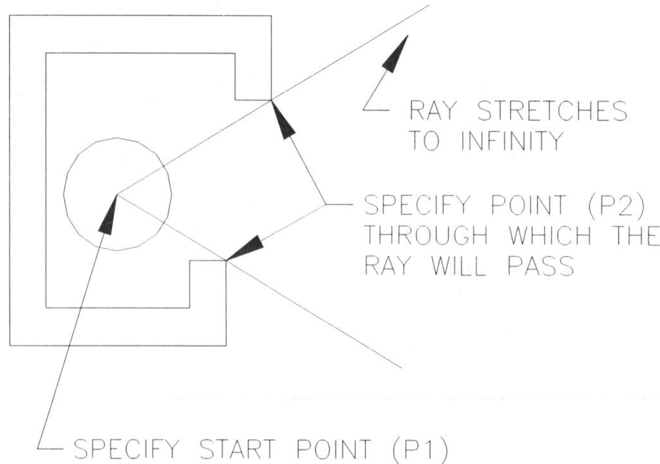

Modify

4.1 Introduction

This chapter covers the changes to the existing modify commands and the addition of new modify commands.

4.2 Old and New

The following are the highlights of the changes to the modify commands. If the changes require elaboration, they will be explained in detail in their own sections.

The commands such as BREAK, EXTEND, FILLET, and TRIM have been enhanced to allow modification to objects in 3 dimensional space despite the Z axis.

The TRIM and EXTEND commands have new options so that you can trim and extend to a boundary that does not physically cross the object to be modified, and the FILLET command now has the ability to create a fillet without trimming away the original objects.

Also, the inquiry commands such as LIST and AREA have been updated to also include the new objects such as spline and ellipse.

Even the property modification commands, such as DDMODIFY and CHPROP, have been updated to include the new individual object linetype scale property.

A new selection method called GROUP has been added to facilitate group selections without the use of blocking.

The EXPLODE command will now explode non-uniformly scaled blocks and a new XPLODE command has been added that allows objects to remain on their inserted layer, after exploding, instead of returning them to their creation layer. This is useful if you have to explode dimensions.

Other changes and additions include new dialog boxes for modifying color and linetype accessed through the new DDCOLOR and DDLTYPE commands.

A new command to change the lengths of objects called LENGTHEN has also been added.

Commands to edit the new objects MTEXT and MLINE have been added called MTPROP and MLEDIT respectively. MLEDIT was explained in Chapter 3 and MTPROP will be explained in Chapter 5.

A brand new feature for modification of text is the SPELL command. This command will check the spelling in an entire drawing. This is also explained in Chapter 5 on Text.

4.3 Modify Properties

With the addition of new objects, the various commands to edit properties have been updated to include those items. The addition of the linetype scale factor that can be applied to every object type has resulted in a modification to the Modify Properties dialog box accessed through the DDMODIFY command. Refer to Figure 4.1 for an illustration of the dialog box for a typical object.

Figure 4.1
Modify Properties dialog box

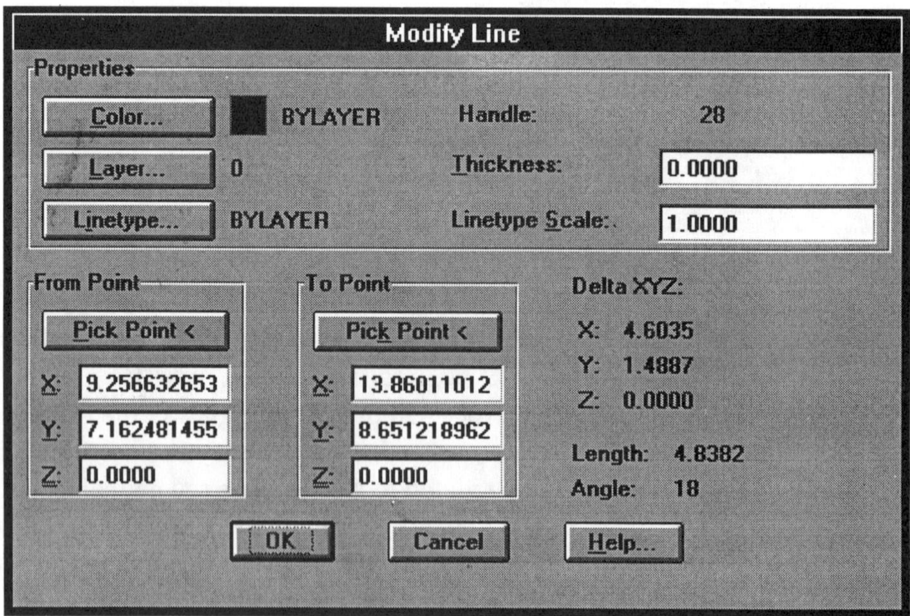

The CHANGE (DDCHPROP) command is used to change properties of multiple objects. Refer to Figure 4.2 for the dialog box.

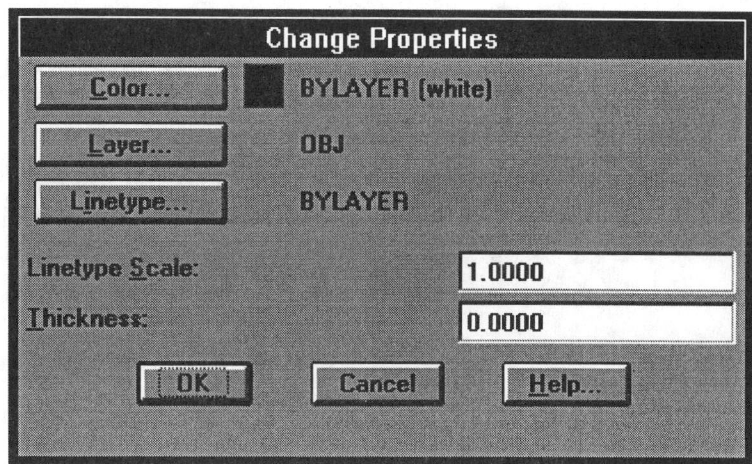

4.4 BREAK Command

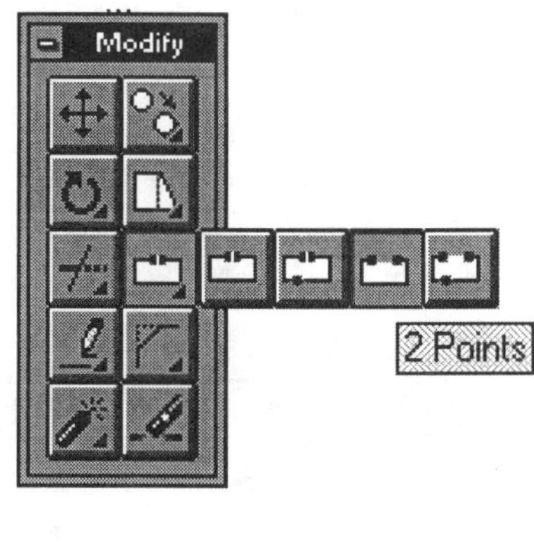

The BREAK command has been enhanced to allow it to work better with 3 Dimensional applications. It will now work on objects even if their direction of extrusion (thickness) is not parallel to the Z axis of the current UCS.   Refer to Figure 4.3.

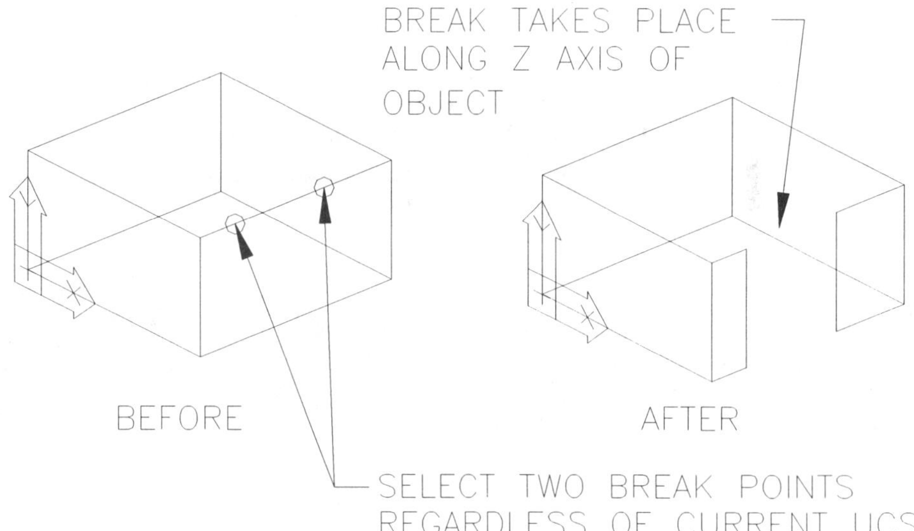

4.5 TRIM Command

There are two new features of the TRIM command - Projection mode and Edge mode. Projection mode is an enhancement for 3 Dimensional modeling and Edge mode is used when the cutting edge does not intersect the object to be trimmed. The following will describe the options in more detail.

Command: **TRIM**
Select cutting edge(s) (Projmode = UCS, Edgemode = Extend)

Project Mode

The Project option specifies the mode or manner which AutoCAD uses when trimming objects. There are three projection modes - None, UCS, and View. Figure 4.4 shows two lines drawn in 3D space. They do not physically intersect. They will be used to explain the projection modes.

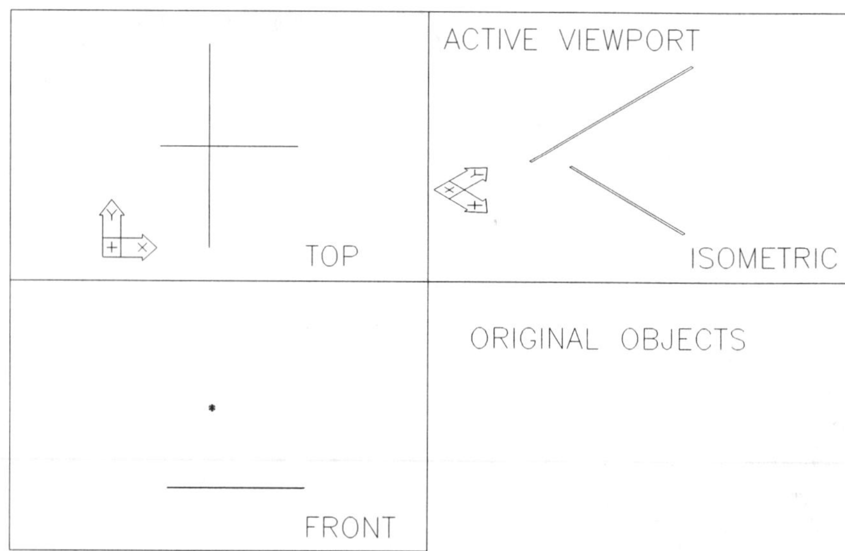

Figure 4.4
Lines in 3D space

None Specifies no projection. AutoCAD trims the objects only if they actually intersect with the cutting edge in 3D space. This is the pre-R13 mode. Refer to Figure 4.5.

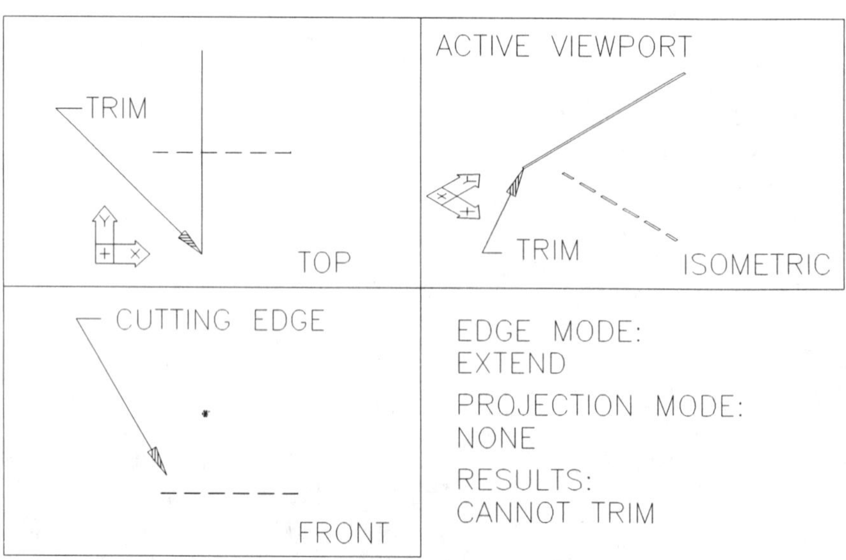

Figure 4.5
Line in 3D space cannot be trimmed using None projection mode

UCS   Specifies projection onto the XY plane of the current UCS. AutoCAD trims objects that do not have to intersect with the cutting edge in 3D space. The objects will be trimmed as long as they appear to intersect if projected onto the XY plane. Refer to Figure 4.6.

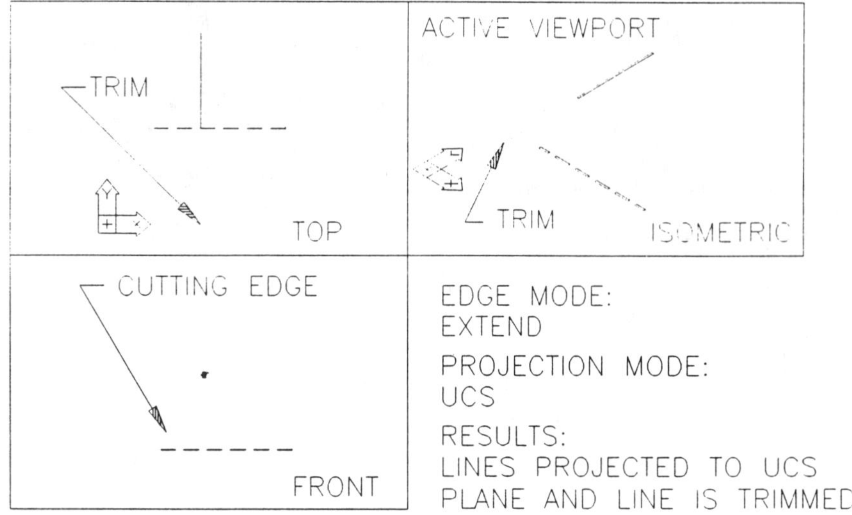

Figure 4.6
Line trimmed in 3D space
using UCS projection mode

View   Specifies projection along the current view direction. Like the UCS option, objects will be trimmed even if they do not intersect with the cutting edge in 3D space. As long as they appear to intersect when they are projected onto the current viewing plane they will be trimmed. Refer to Figure 4.7.

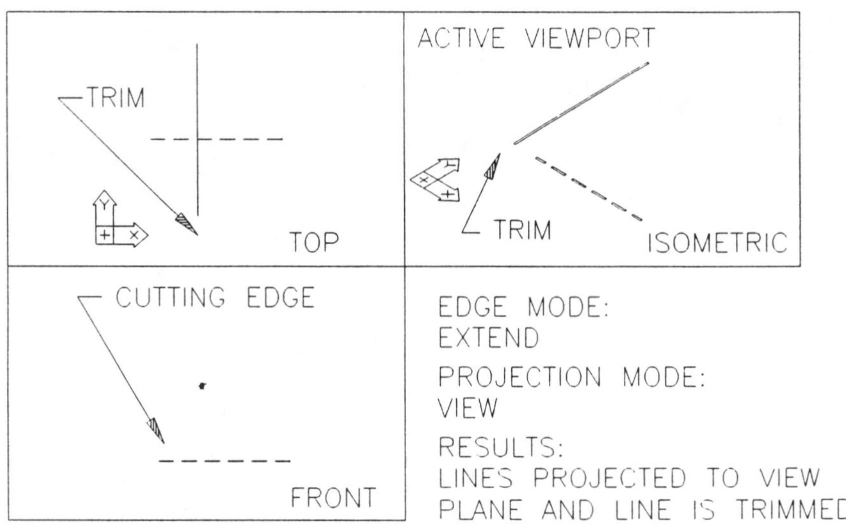

Figure 4.7
Line trimmed in 3D space
using View projection mode

Edge

The Edge option determines whether objects are trimmed where another object explicitly crosses (intersects) or if another object crossing can be implied. The two Edge modes are Extend and No extend.

No extend   This mode is the pre-R13 mode. An object will only be trimmed if the cutting edge actually intersects the object to be trimmed.

Extend   This mode uses implied intersection by extending the cutting edge along the natural path of the cutting edge object until it intersects with the object to be trimmed. Refer to Figure 4.8.

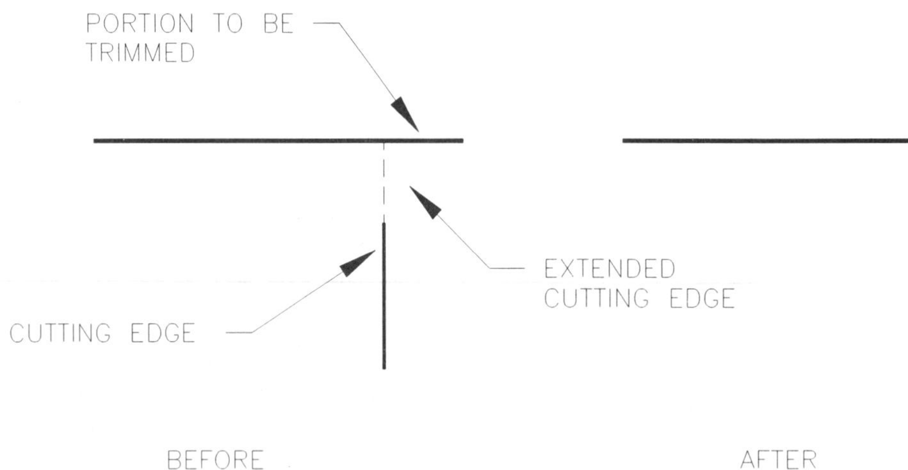

4.6 EXTEND Command

The two new features (Projection mode and Edge mode) that have been added to the TRIM command have also been added to the EXTEND command. Projection mode is an enhancement for 3 Dimensional modeling and Edge mode is used when the cutting edge does not intersect with the object to be trimmed. Refer to Section 4.7 for an explanation and example of the projection mode. Figure 4.9 will illustrate the Edge mode for Extending.

Command: **EXTEND**
Select boundary edge(s) (Projmode = UCS, Edgemode = Extend)

Figure 4.9
Extending line to meet implied
boundary edge

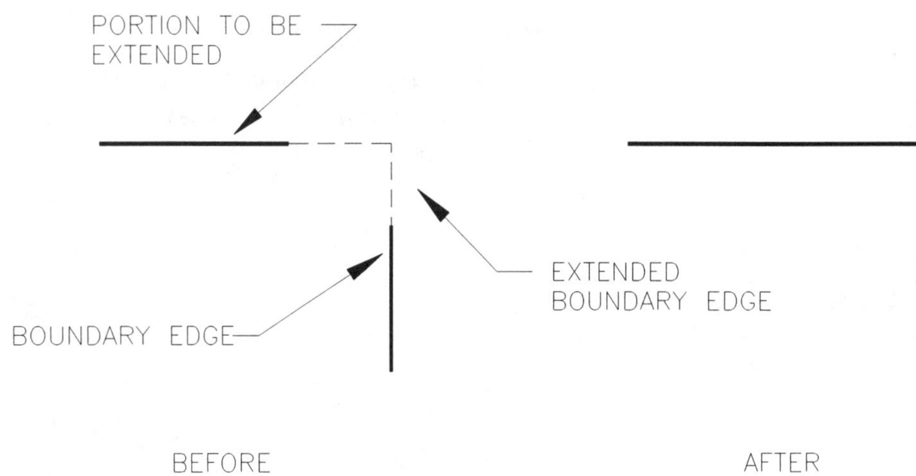

4.7 FILLET Command

The FILLET command has three new features - working in 3 dimensions,
working on 3D Solids, and a Trim mode.

Command: **FILLET**
(TRIM mode) Current fillet radius = 0.5
Polyline/Radius/Trim <Select first object>:

Working in 3 Dimensions
The FILLET command will now fillet lines and other objects in 3D space
regardless of the orientation of the current UCS or the plane upon which the
object was created. Refer to Figure 4.10.

Figure 4.10
Filleting in 3D space

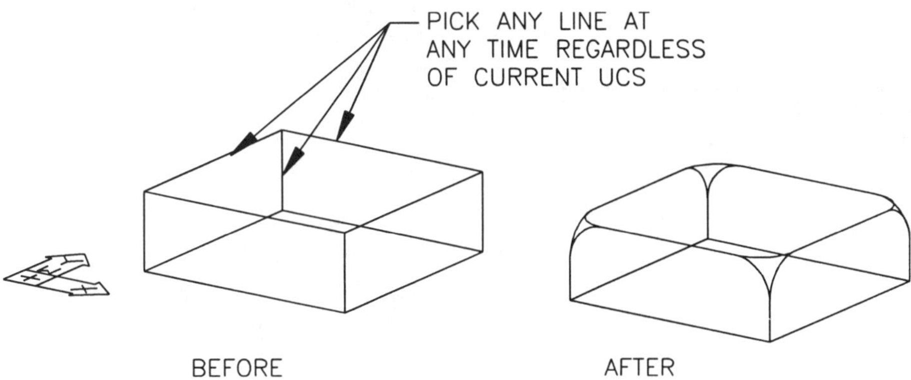

Working on 3D Solids

The FILLET command will now fillet 3D solids because 3D solids have now been integrated into AutoCAD. Figure 4.11 shows the application of filleting on a 3D solid.

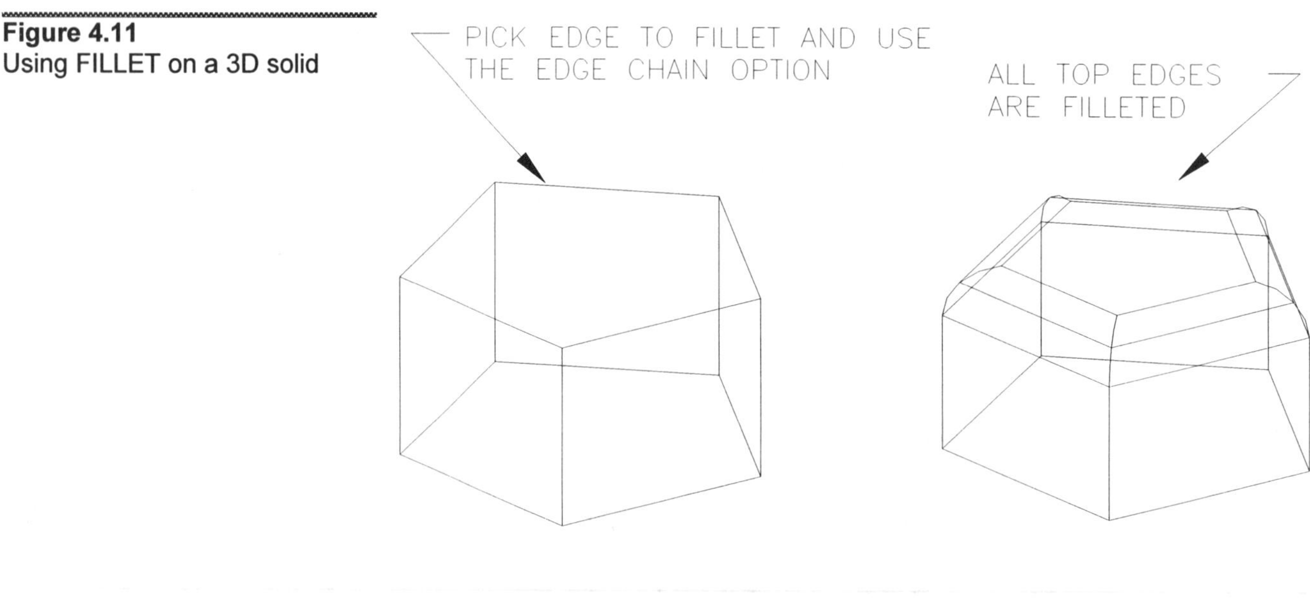

Trim Mode

The FILLET command now has the option of trimming (and extending) objects or leaving them as is when the fillet is applied. Figure 4.12 shows the application of filleting using trim and no trim modes.

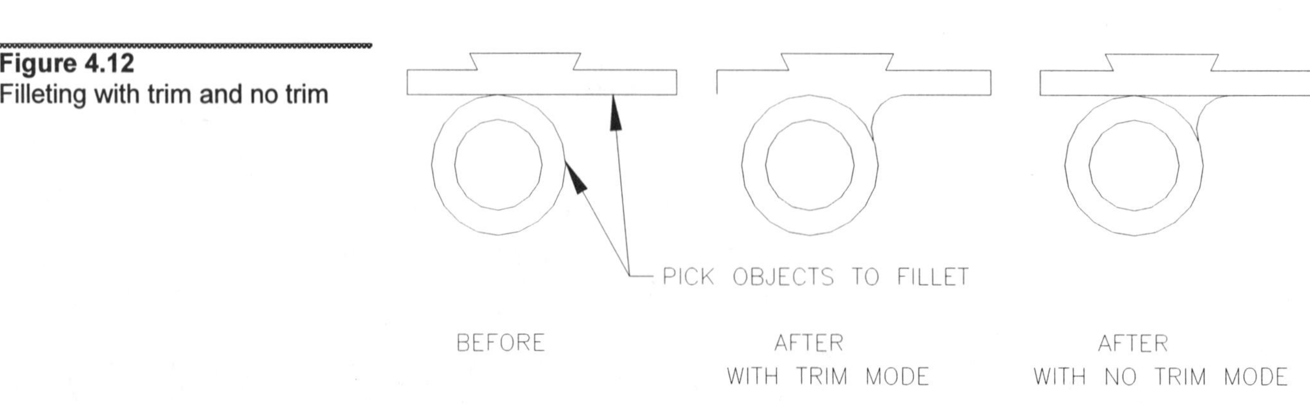

The GROUP command allows the user to link objects by a common name. The Group tool is found in the standard toolbar. Groups can be thought of as named selection sets. In this way, you can quickly select a group of objects by name to perform any type of modification. Groups help organize a drawing into named collections of objects. When objects are grouped, you can act upon them by specifying their name, or by picking on a single object that is contained in a group. When a named group is copied, the copy becomes an unnamed group. An unnamed group is a group that is linked together but does not have a formal name. AutoCAD assigns a letter and number to "unnamed" groups as they are created such as A1 or A2. A dialog box is used to create, identify, and modify groups. Refer to Figure 4.13 for the dialog box and the following for a description of the box's contents.

Figure 4.13
Object Grouping dialog box

Group Name

This area contains a listing of all the named (and unnamed) groups. The first column represents the group name and the second column denotes whether the group is selectable. If a group is selectable, when you pick one element in the group, all the elements are selected to be acted upon.

Group Identification

This area is used to identify a group in the drawing or to enter the name of a new group.

Group Name   If you highlight a group, either from the list or by using the Find Name button, the group name will appear in the box. This box is also used when you want to name a new group.

Description   You can add a 64-character description to further identify a group.

Find Name   Finds the name of a group in the drawing. When the button is pressed, the drawing screen returns and you are asked to pick an object on the drawing. If it is a named group, it will be displayed.

Highlight   If you have highlighted a group name and pick this button, every object that is linked by that group name will be highlighted on the drawing.

Include Unnamed   Used to access all the unnamed groups in the drawing. When it is checked, the "unnamed" group names appear in the list.

Create Group

This area is used to create new groups.

New   Creates a new group. You will be prompted to identify the objects in the drawing that will be added to the group.

Selectable   Identifies whether a new group will be selectable or unselectable upon creation.

Unnamed   This check box is used to create a new group that will be unnamed.

Change Group

This area is used to make changes to the objects in a group.

Remove   Used to remove objects from a group.

Add   Used to add objects to a group.

Rename   Used to rename a group.

Re-order   Used to re-order the objects in a group.

Description   Used to add a description to a group.

Explode	Used to remove all the objects from a group and to remove the group name also.
Selectable	Used to toggle a group from selectable to non-selectable, or to do the reverse.

Groups and the Drawing Aids Dialog Box

There is a group check box in the Drawing Aids dialog box. Its purpose is to make groups selectable or unselectable globally. If the box is checked, then the behavior of the group is governed by the Object Grouping dialog box. If the box is not checked, groups are not selectable, regardless of their normal status. Refer to Figure 4.14.

Figure 4.14
Drawing Aids dialog box
showing Groups box checked

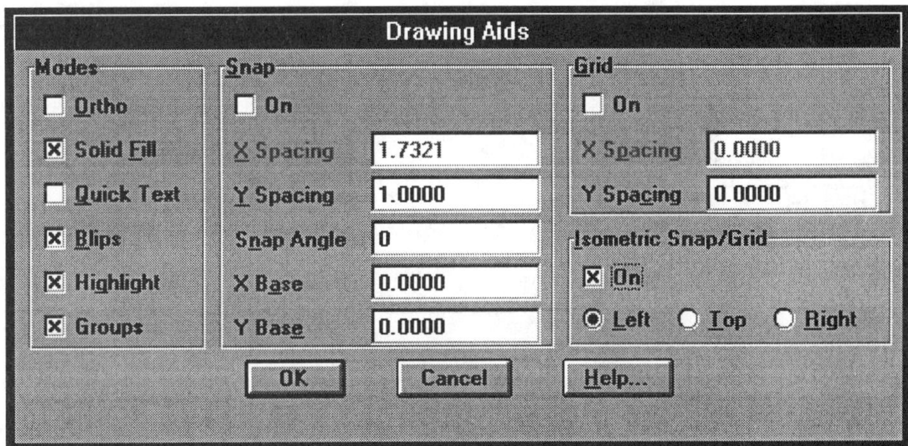

4.9 LENGTHEN Command

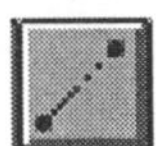

The LENGTHEN command allows you to increase or decrease the length of lines or arcs. You can enter specific values or draw the object dynamically. This tool can be found under the Stretch flyout in the Modify toolbar. The following text explains the command and its options:

Command: **LENGTHEN**
DElta/Percent/Total/DYnamic/<Select Object>:

DElta	Changes length by specifying an incremental length, measured from the endpoint of the selected object closest to the pick point. A negative value trims the object. If you use the Angle suboption, you can control the length of an arc by a delta angle in degrees. Refer to Figure 4.15.

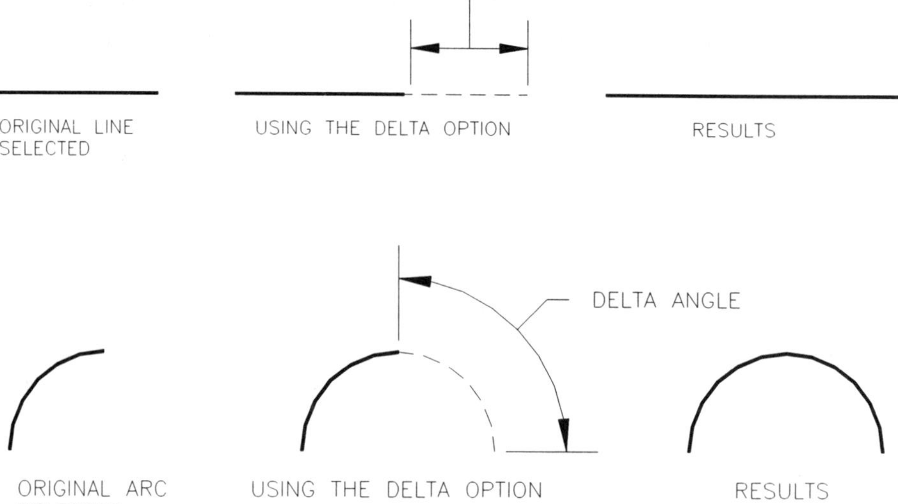

Figure 4.15
LENGTHEN command using the Delta option

Percent   Changes the length by specifying a percentage of its total length. Greater than 100% increases, while less than 100% decreases. Refer to Figure 4.16.

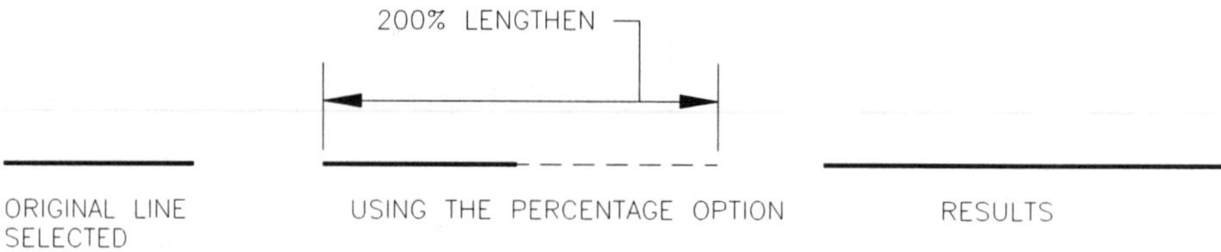

Figure 4.16
LENGTHEN command using the Percentage option

Total   Changes the length by entering the actual desired length or, in the case of an arc, the total included angle. Refer to Figure 4.17.

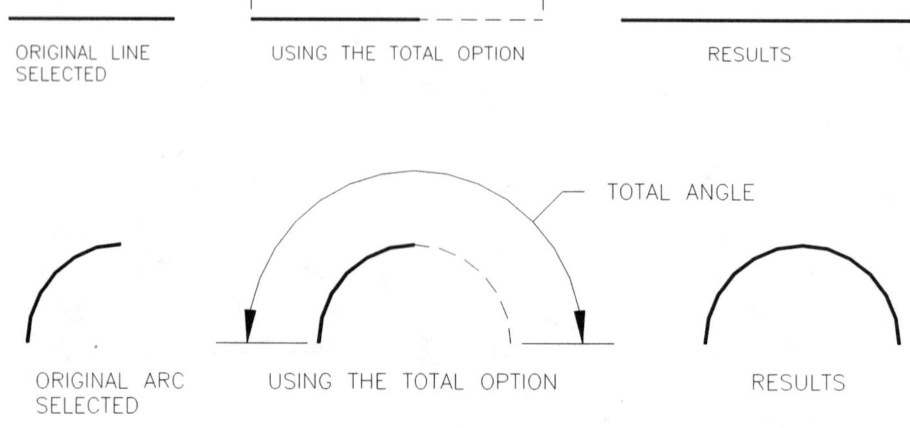

Figure 4.17
LENGTHEN command using the Total option

DYnamic   This final option of the LENGTHEN command allows you
to drag the object to the desired size.

CHAPTER 5

Text

5.1 Introduction

This chapter will explain the changes to the commands relating to text. There are three main changes: the addition of a new text object called MText, the addition of a spell checker, and the support of True Type fonts.

5.2 Multiline Text

If you want to create a single line of text, the TEXT and DTEXT commands are still available to you for this purpose. However, if you want to enter a paragraph of text, the new MTEXT command is the command to use.

The MTEXT command will create a paragraph of text that will be treated as a single object. The paragraph of MText fits within a specified width, but can be indefinite in length, it has enhanced editing options compared to the original TEXT object and you can apply different fonts, color, and/or text heights to individual words or phrases within the paragraph.

Using MTEXT

The following is the initial command description and its options.

Command: **MTEXT**
Attach/Rotation/Style/Height/Direction/<Insertion point>: **pick a start point to define one corner of the paragraph boundary or enter an option**
Attach/Rotation/Style/Direction/Width/2Points/<other corner>: **pick other corner of the boundary or enter an option**

The following is an explanation of the options:

Attach   Sets the anchor point on the paragraph of text. You are presented with suboptions from which to choose.

Rotation   Sets the rotation angle of the paragraph of text.

Style   Sets the style of text.

Height   Sets the height of uppercase text.

Direction   Sets the direction the text will travel - Horizontal or Vertical.

Width   Sets the width (in units) of the paragraph of text, which will control the justification.

2Points   Sets the width by specifying two points.

Once you have specified the boundary of the MText paragraph, you are transferred to a text editor. If you use the MTEXT command within the DOS version of AutoCAD, you will be automatically transferred to a DOS text editor. Refer to Figure 5.1. By default the DOS version uses the EDIT program supplied with DOS. The type of DOS text editor used can be set using the MTEXTED system variable.

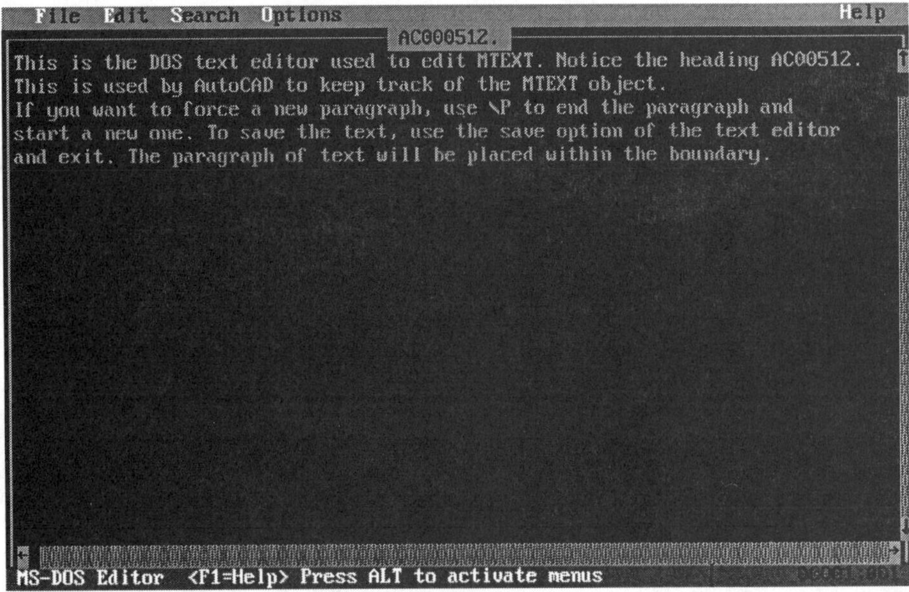

Figure 5.1
DOS text editor used to enter MText

If you are using the Windows version, you are transferred to the Edit MText dialog box. It contains more options for formatting the paragraph of text. Refer to Figure 5.2.

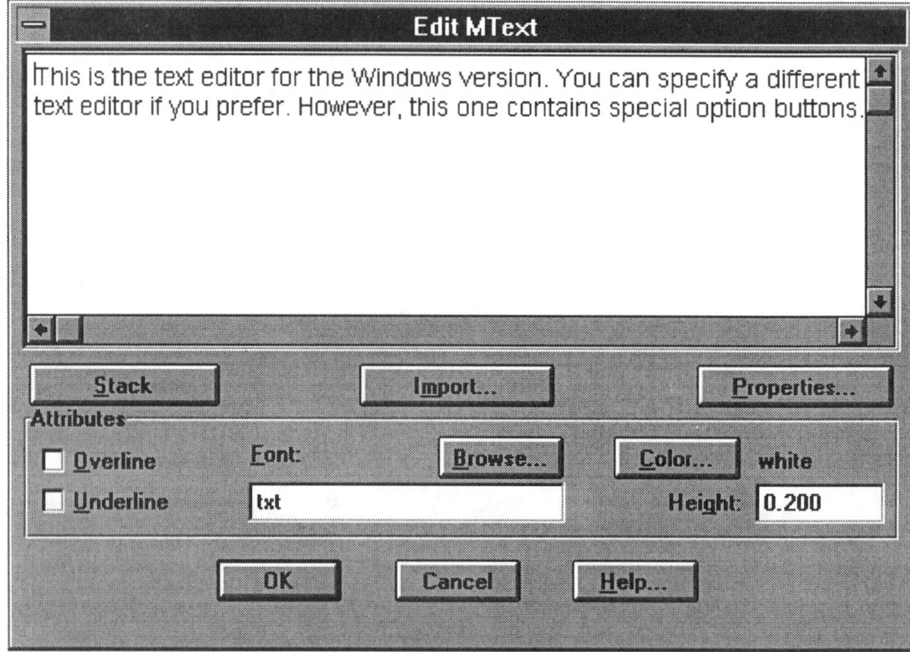

Edit MText Dialog Box

The following is a description of the areas within the Edit MText dialog box.

Text box   Displays the entered text.

Stack   Creates text that is aligned vertically or stacked upon each other.

Import   Displays the Import Text File dialog box used to bring in a text file and place it with the text boundary.

Properties   Displays the MText Properties dialog box. This dialog box will be explained later.

Attributes   This area contains the various attribute features as follows:

   Overline   Turns on overlining for new or selected text.

   Underline   Turns on underlining for new or selected text.

   Font   Specifies a font for new or selected text.

Browse   Displays the Change Font dialog box, in which you specify a font file. This only works on highlighted text. Refer to Figure 5.3.

Color   Specifies a color for new or selected text. If you pick on the Color button, a dialog box is displayed from which to choose the color. Refer to Figure 5.4.

Height   Specifies the height for new or selected text.

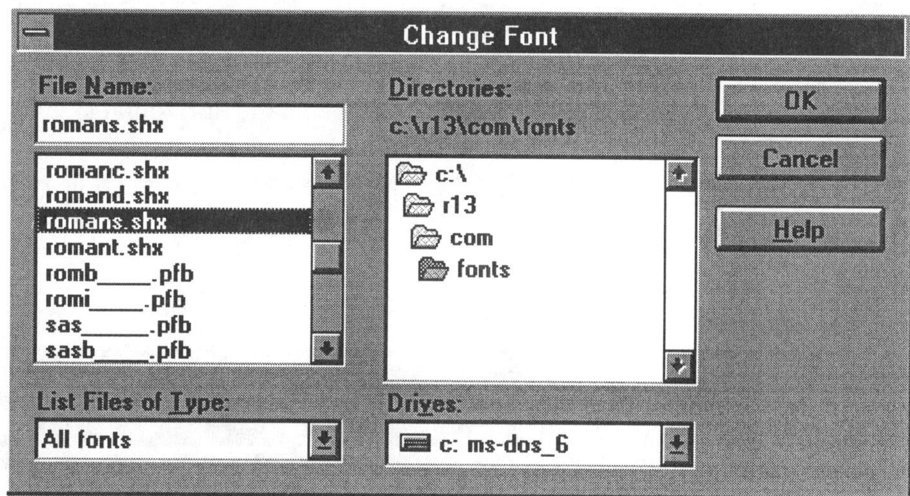

Figure 5.3
Change Font dialog box

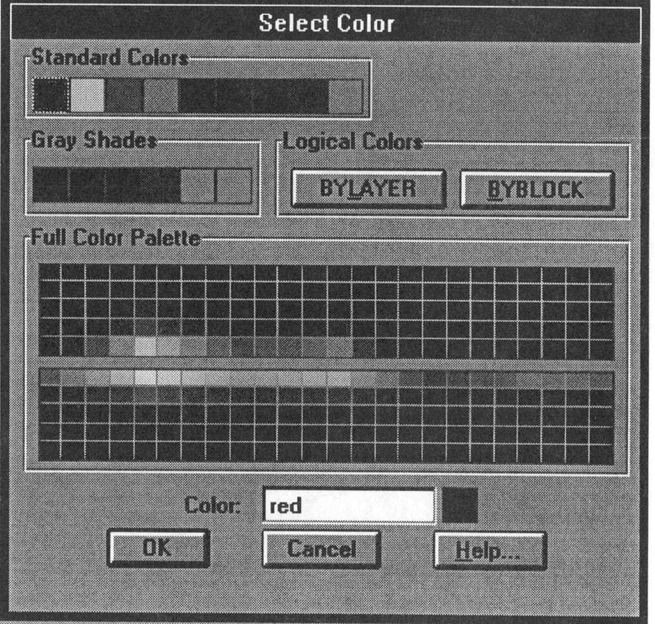

Figure 5.4
Select Color dialog box

MText Properties Dialog Box

The following is a description of the areas within the MText Properties dialog box. Refer to Figure 5.5.

Text Style   Sets the text style to be used for the new paragraph of text.

Text Height   Sets the default text height for the paragraph of text.

Direction   Sets the direction from which the text will be read. English and Spanish are read horizontally, while Chinese and Japanese text is sometimes read vertically.

Attachment   Sets the text boundary alignment and direction of text spill.

Width   Sets the horizontal size of the text boundary.

Rotation   Sets the rotation angle of the text boundary.

Figure 5.5
MText Properties dialog box

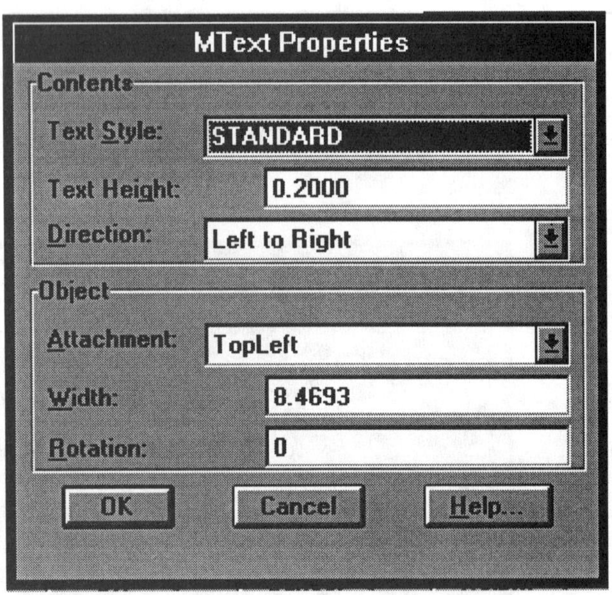

5.3 MText Modifications

Once you have entered MText and placed the paragraph on the drawing, you can modify it in one of two ways. The first edits the text itself. The second adjusts the properties of the MText.

To edit a paragraph of MText, use the DDEDIT command as you would on standard single line text. Instead of the single line Edit Text dialog box, AutoCAD displays the full feature Edit MText dialog box for the Windows version or the DOS Editor for the DOS version.

MText Properties

To make changes to the MText properties of a paragraph, use the MTPROP command. Once you have selected the paragraph to edit, the MText Properties dialog box will appear as shown in Figure 5.5.

5.4 Spelling Check

Spell checking has been introduced for the first time in AutoCAD R13. The command to invoke it is called, appropriately, SPELL. Whether it is in a TEXT object string or in an MTEXT object string, the spelling utility will check each word against the items in the current dictionary. When you select the SPELL command and select the text to check, you are presented with the Check Spelling dialog box that appears in Figure 5.6.

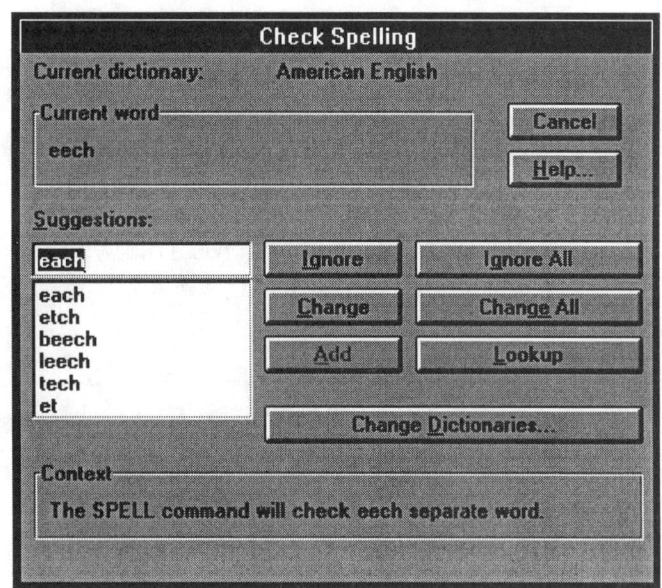

Figure 5.6
Check Spelling dialog box

The bottom line in the dialog box displays the line of text AutoCAD is currently checking; the top of the dialog box shows the word AutoCAD is currently checking. In this case, AutoCAD is checking the word *eech*, which is incorrect. The spelling utility looks up the closest words alphabetically to the word *eech*. At the top of the list is *each*. To replace *eech* with *each*, pick either the Change button or the Change All button.

The Change button replaces the indicated word; the Change All button replaces all occurrences of the word in the drawing.

You can change dictionaries to those in other languages, enter customized dictionaries designed specifically for your discipline, or add new words to the current dictionary that may be of significance to your work. You can also ignore words that the dictionary cannot locate but you know to be correct, such as names of people and locations.

The following is further explanation on the areas of the Check Spelling dialog box.

Suggestions	Displays the word being checked and lists the alternatives from which to choose.
Ignore	Skips the word currently being checked.
Ignore All	Skips all the remaining words that match the current word being checked.
Lookup	Checks the spelling of the word in the Suggestions box. You can enter a word in the upper Suggestions box to be checked and then pick the Lookup button.

5.5 New Fonts

Fonts control the shape of the letters of text. The usual procedure to use a font is to create a Text Style using the STYLE command and assign a font, such as ROMANS.SHX, to it. This has not changed it R13. What has changed is the ability to use TrueType and Adobe Type 1 PostScript fonts in addition to AutoCAD's own shape fonts.

Font File Extensions	
Font Type	**File Extension**
AutoCAD	.shx
TrueType	.ttf
Type 1 (PostScript)	.pfa (ASCII) or .pfb (binary)

There are many TrueType and Adobe Type 1 PostScript fonts available from third-party vendors (those who sell products other than

AutoCAD). Once you have installed a new set of fonts, add their directory to the AutoCAD library search path specified by the ACAD environment variable.

Text that uses a Text Style that contains TrueType or Type 1 fonts will be displayed using that particular font. However, AutoCAD usually displays the PostScript font in outline only - on the screen and during a plot. This is controlled by the TEXTFILL system variable. If it is set to 0, only the outline is shown. If it is set to 1, then the appropriate fill is used.

CHAPTER 6

Dimensions

6.1 Introduction

The fundamentals of dimensioning drawings has not changed from R12 to R13. What has changed is the way you access dimension commands, the procedure to set up dimension styles, and the addition of some new commands. This chapter will explain the changes to the commands relating to dimensioning.

6.2 Old and New

This section will introduce you to some of the major changes with dimensioning, giving you a quick background. These changes will be explained in more detail in their own sections.

Direct Commands

In keeping with making the transition from one version to a new version an easier step, AutoCAD has kept the pre-R13 method of using the dimension command. You can enter the DIM command on the command line and enter the dimension command options, such as Horizontal or Leader, and make use of the pre-R13 dimensioning features. However, the R13 dimensioning features have made access to dimensioning commands more streamlined, with direct command usage, such as DIMLINEAR to perform either horizontal or vertical dimensioning.

In the Windows version of AutoCAD, a new toolbar has been created for easy access to the dimension commands.

Dimension Styles

The Dimension Styles still exist but the creation and access to Dimension

Styles has been revamped with additional capabilities including more dimension variables to control new features. A couple of the new features that you should be aware of early on are the setting of Units for dimensioning and the setting of Text Styles for dimensioning. Both are independent of the current units and current text style.

However it should be noted that the current drawing unit and unit precision do affect the manner in which values are entered for the various dimension variables. For example, if you set your units to fractions and the precision to 1/4, you will not be able to enter dimension variable values less that 1/4 of a unit. This has not changed from previous versions but it is important to remember the fact.

Geometric Tolerancing

Tolerancing of geometric features has been in use for the manufacturing industry for a long time now. But its use has been on the increase, especially with the increased use of Computer Aided Machining and Robotics. AutoCAD can now apply geometric tolerancing.

6.3   Dimension Drawing Commands

There are a variety of dimension types available, each with its own particular use. Refer to Figure 6.1 for the Definition points and Figure 6.2 for typical dimensions. Previously, the DIM command was used to access dimension commands. This method is still available but has been superseded by direct dimension commands such as DIMLINEAR.

Figure 6.1
Dimension Definition points

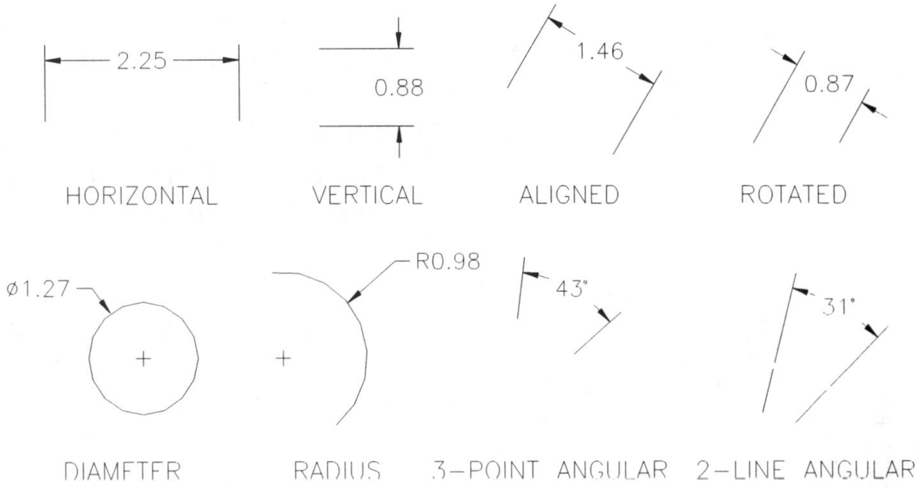

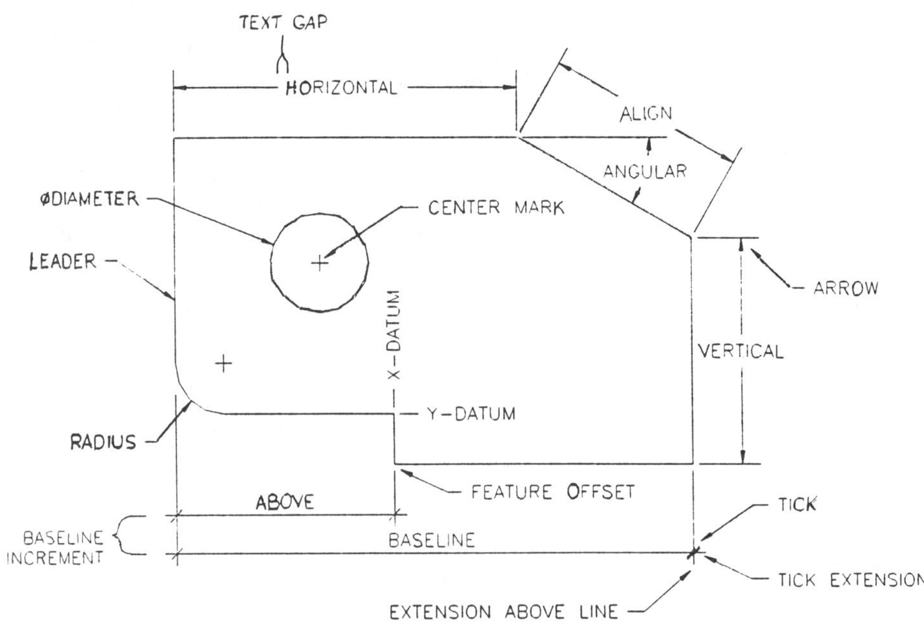

Figure 6.2
Typical dimensions showing AutoCAD terminology

What follows is a list of the pull-down menu dimension selections (DOS and Windows Full menu) and the dimension types available under each. With the Windows version, you have access to the Dimension toolbar available from the Tools/Toolbars pull-down menu. The direct dimension commands are shown in parentheses.

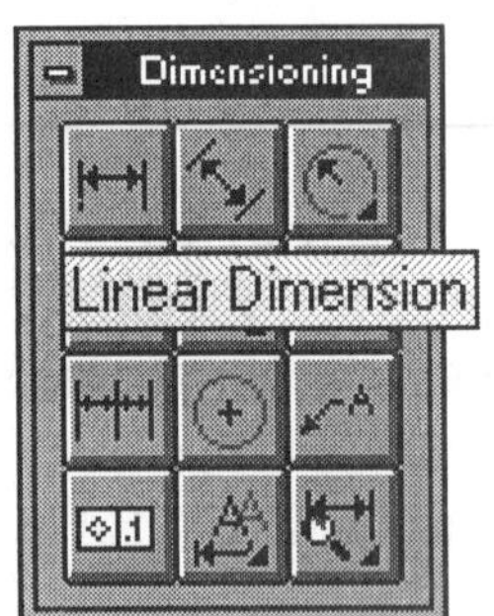

LINEAR (DIMLINEAR)

Horizontal command option: Dimension with a dimension line aligned to the X axis.
Vertical command option: Dimension with a dimension line aligned to the Y axis.
Rotated command option: Dimension with a dimension line drawn at a specific angle.

ALIGNED (DIMALIGNED)

Dimensions with a dimension line parallel to the two extension defining pick points.

RADIAL

Radius submenu selection (DIMRADIUS): Dimension used to specify a radius of a circle or an arc.
Diameter submenu selection (DIMDIAMETER): Dimension used to specify the diameter of a circle or an arc.

ANGULAR (DIMANGULAR)

Creates an angular dimension.

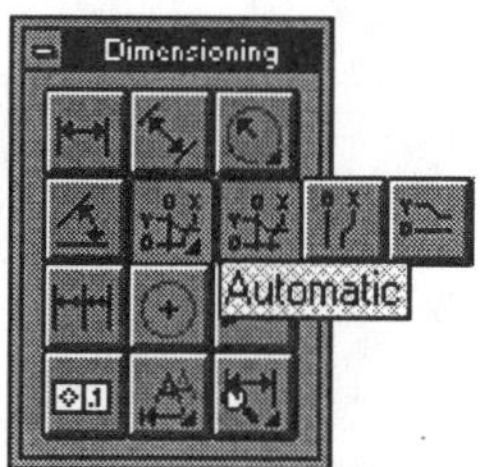

ORDINATE (DIMORDINATE)

Automatic submenu selection: Dimension used to specify the X or Y coordinate location feature (coordinate point) based on the 0,0 location of the current UCS. The X or Y coordinate is extracted depending on the orientation of the leader line. The leader line extends from the selected feature to the dimensioned text.

X-Datum submenu selection: Dimension used to specify the X location of a feature based on the 0,0 location of the current UCS. The text is placed at the end of the leader.

Y-Datum submenu selection: Dimension used to specify the Y location of a feature based on the 0,0 location of the current UCS. The text is placed at the end of the leader.

BASELINE (DIMBASELINE)

Used to dimension several features from a common starting or base point. It is used in succession each time a new dimension is required.

CONTINUE (DIMCONTINUE)

Used to dimension several features that are in line using a chaining, or linked together, dimension. Used in succession, each time a new dimension is required.

CENTER MARK (DIMCENTER)

Creates a center mark or centerlines inside a circle or an arc.

LEADER (LEADER)

Creates leader line segments with an arrow at one end and Text or MText at the other. You can also set the format that will be used, such as splines versus straight lines, and blocks instead of text on the end of the leader line.

TOLERANCE (TOLERANCE)

Creates symbols for geometric tolerancing.

OBLIQUE (DIMEDIT)

Modifies extension line to be drawn at oblique angles to the dimension line.

ALIGN TEXT (DIMTEDIT)

Modifies the alignment of dimension text.

This section describes the procedure to use the six common dimensioning commands: Linear Horizontal, Radial Diameter, Ordinate X-Datum, Angular 3-Point, Leader, and Center Marks.

Linear Horizontal

Refer to Figure 6.3 to see the results of this command.

Command: **DIMLINEAR**

First extension line origin or <Enter> to select: **pick a start point for the extension line** (If you press <Enter>, you can select a line, an arc, or a circle to automatically measure.)

Second extension line origin: **pick the start point for the second extension line** (Both points are used to calculate the measured length. This prompt will not be displayed if an object was measured automatically.)

Dimension line location (Text/Angle/Horizontal/Vertical/Rotated): **pick a location on the drawing through which the dimension line will be drawn.** (If you enter T, you can customize the dimension text; entering A, however, will set the rotation angle of the dimension text. Entering an Hor V forces the dimension to be either horizontal or vertical. Entering an R allows you to enter an angle to which the extension and dimension lines are rotated.)

Figure 6.3
Linear horizontal dimension

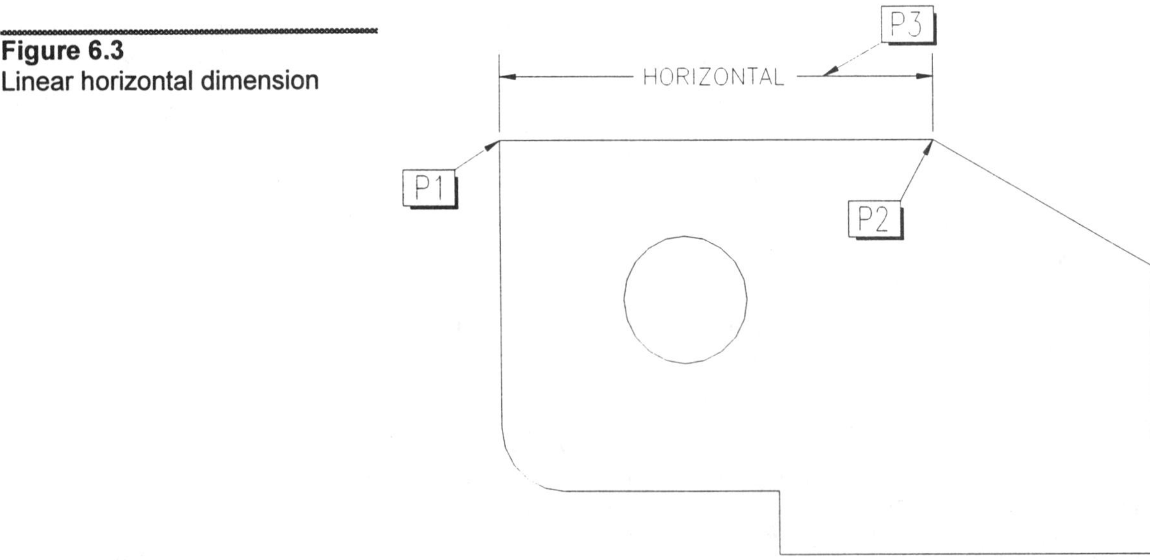

Radial Diameter

Refer to Figure 6.4 to see the results of this command.

Command: **DIMDIAMETER**
Select arc or circle: **pick a location along the curve** (The point you
  pick will be used as the location through which the leader line will
  be drawn.)
Dimension line location (Text/Angle): **pick a location for the end
  of the leader line** (If you enter a T, you can enter specific text;
  entering an A, however, allows you to rotate the text to a set angle.)

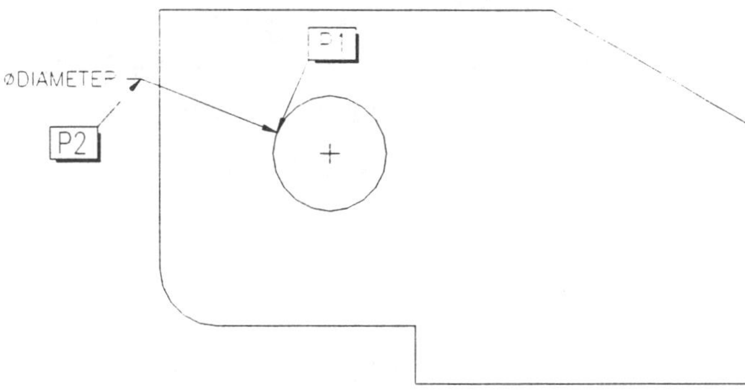

Figure 6.4
Radial diameter dimension

Ordinate X-Datum

Refer to Figure 6.5 to see the results of this command.

Command: **DIMORDINATE**
Select Feature: **pick a coordinate location**
Leader end point (X datum/Y datum/ Text): **pick a location along
  the Y axis** (If you pick along the X axis, the Y coordinate is
  extracted. If you pick along the Y axis, the X coordinate is
  extracted. To force a particular coordinate extraction, use one of the
  datum options. Use T to enter text.)

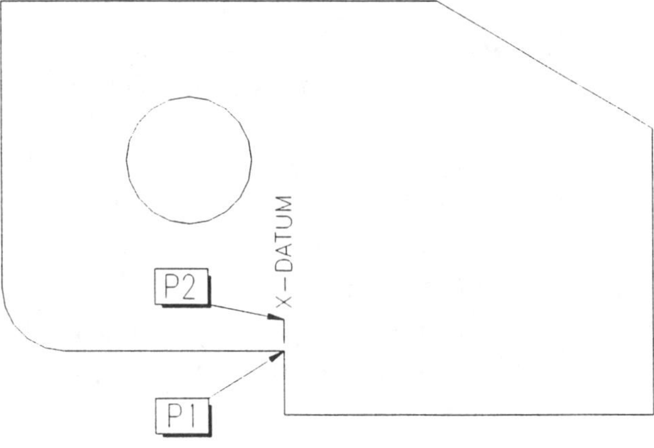

Figure 6.5
Ordinate X-datum dimension

Angular 3-Point

Refer to Figure 6.6 to see the results of this command.

Command: **DIMANGULAR**
Select arc, circle, line, or return: **press <Enter> for the 3-point method.** (If you select an arc, a circle, or a line, AutoCAD will extract the rotation angle from the object.)
Angle vertex: **pick the point where the angle converges**
First angle endpoint: **pick a point that defines the first axis line, extending from the vertex**
Second angle endpoint: **pick a point that defines the second axis line, extending from the vertex**
Dimension arc line location (Text/Angle): **pick a location through which the dimension arc will pass**

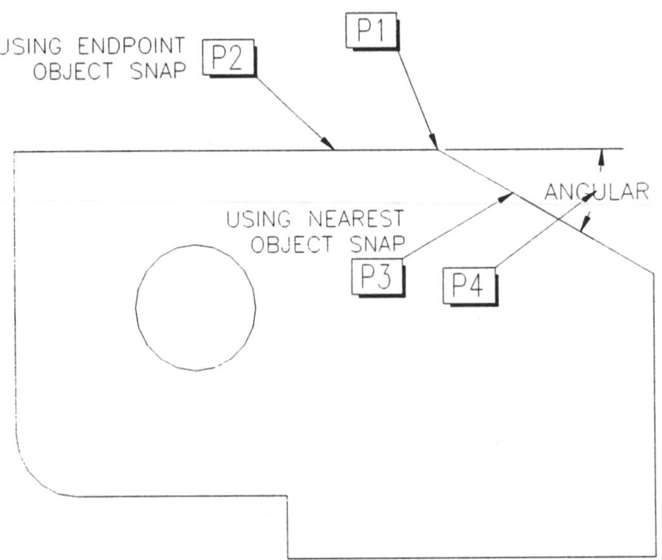

Figure 6.6
Angular 3-point dimension

Leader

Refer to Figure 6.7 to see the results of this command.

Command: **LEADER**
From point: **pick the location for the point of the arrowhead**
To point (Format/ Annotation/ Undo)<Annotation>: **pick a location for the end of the leader line** (For the last entry, you can pick as many points as you like. When finished picking points, press <Enter> to move on.)

The following is the list of the options and their purpose:

Format   Controls how the leader lines are drawn. You can have a spline or straight lines, arrow or none.

Annotation   Controls what will appear at the note end of the leader line. You can enter a single line of text or more options such as geometric tolerance symbols, existing leader note copies, blocks, no annotation, or MText for multiple lines of text.

Undo   Backs up one step in the creation of the leader line.

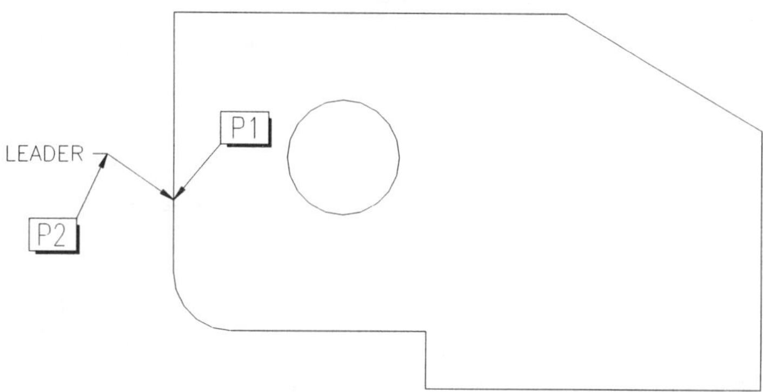

Figure 6.7
Leader

Center Marks

Refer to Figure 6.8 to see the results of this command.

Command: **DIMCENTER**
Select circle or arc: **pick the edge of the curve and AutoCAD will place a center mark at the center of the curve**

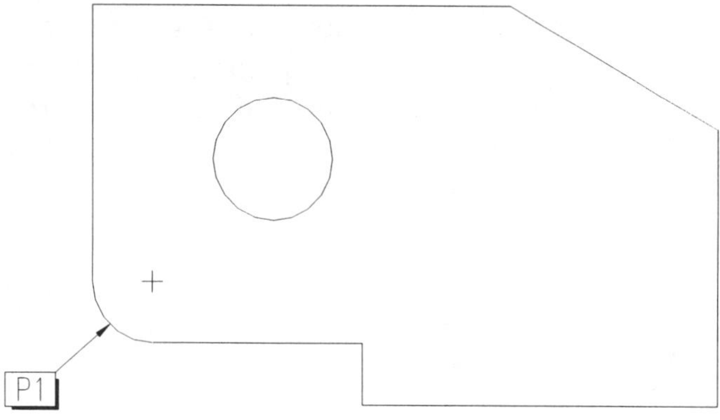

Figure 6.8
Center mark

6.5   Editing Dimensions

When you wish to make changes to a dimension, AutoCAD has several new utilities for this purpose.

For instance, when you want to make a change that will be reflected in all the dimensions of a particular type, modify the dimension style settings using the DDIM command to access the Dimension Style dialog box. Changes in the settings will be automatically reflected in all the dimensions that use that style. Refer to Section 6.6 on Dimension Styles.

The DIMEDIT Command

The DIMEDIT command changes text. Its options are as follows:

Home — Returns the selected text to its orginal default position.

New — Allows changes to the value associative dimensions. You simply enter the new value and then pick the dimensions to change. To return to the original calculated value, enter a blank line for the new text.

Rotate — Rotates the text value to any angle.

Oblique — This option draws the extension lines obliquely (at an angle) to the feature to be dimensioned, instead of perpendicularly. The dimension line stays parallel to the feature.

The DIMTEDIT Command

The DIMTEDIT command is used to change the position of text along the dimension line. The following are the options and the results:

Left — Moves the text to the left end of the dimension line.
Right — Moves the text to the right end of the dimension line.
Home — Moves the text to the original home position.
Angle — Moves the text to an entered angle.

6.6   Dimension Styles

The key to effectively controlling the appearance of your dimensions is to have control over the dimension variables that effect this display. Just like text styles that control the appearance of text, dimension styles control the appearance of dimensions. Dimension styles group together a combination

of the dimension variable settings under a descriptive name to keep track of different combinations. For example, when dimensioning a mechanical drawing, select the preset dimension style for mechanical; the same applies for architectural dimensions. You can have as many different combinations as you desire by creating new styles from old ones and giving them a new name and new settings.

Creating Dimension Styles

Select the Data/Dimension Style pull-down menu (or use the DDIM command) and you are presented with a dialog box similar to the one in Figure 6.9. At the top of the box, is the Dimension Style area. In this area, next to the title Current, is a pop-up list of previously created dimension styles that are contained within the current drawing. If you are just starting to create dimension styles, then the current style will be called "STANDARD". Each dimension you create would have this style associated with it. To create a new style, enter its name in the "Name:" entry box. It will initially be a duplicate of the current dimension style.

Figure 6.9
Dimension Styles dialog box

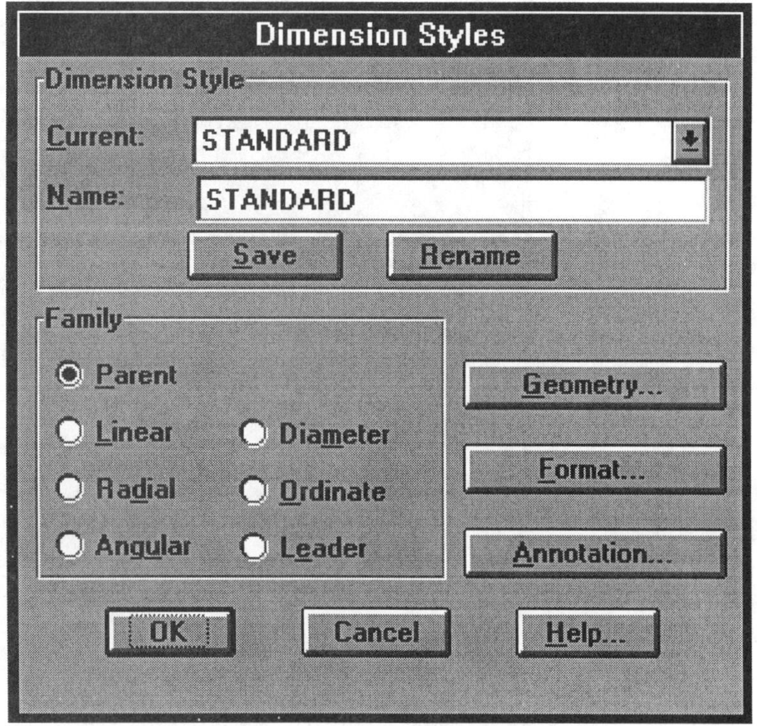

To change the settings of a dimension style, refer to the Family area. This area has the following radio buttons: Parent, Linear, Radial, Angular, Diameter, Ordinate, and Leader. These buttons allow you to make global settings for a particular style using the Parent button, and individual settings for the other buttons. To create a new style, make general settings using the Parent button and then create individual differences using the other buttons. In this way, you can have one style name while having individual differences for different dimension types, such as linear and leader. For an architectural dimension style, use tick marks for linear dimensions and arrowheads for leader lines. This can be accomplished under one dimension style. To change settings, select one of the three buttons labeled: Geometry, Format, or Annotation. These are explained in the following sections. Remember to use the Save button whenever you make modifications to a dimension style. These changes will be reflected in all the dimensions that use the modified style.

Geometry Dialog Box

The Geometry dialog box, under the Dimension Styles dialog box, controls the appearance of the dimension lines, extension lines, arrowheads, center marks, and scale of the dimension features. Refer to Figure 6.10.

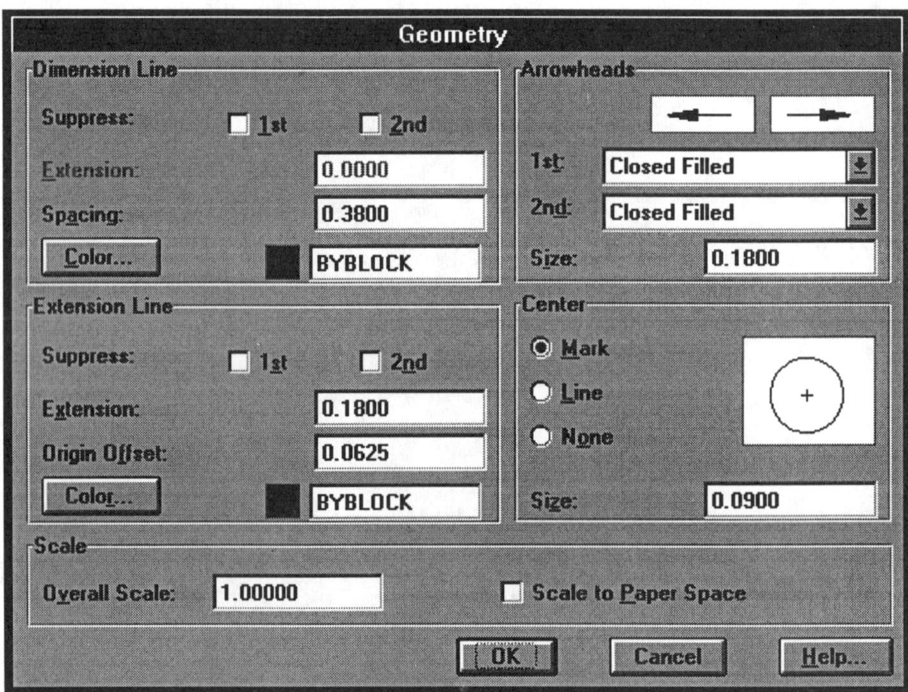

The following explains each area in the dialog box. The dimension variable controlled is shown in brackets.

Dimension Line

Suppress 1st and 2nd (DIMSD1, DIMSD2)
These boxes are used to suppress the drawing of either or both dimension lines.

Extension (DIMDLE)
This box is only available with certain arrowhead types. It is used to extend the dimension line past the extension line. Commonly

used for architectural dimensions using oblique arrowhead marks.

Spacing (DIMDLI)
This is used to control the stacking of dimension lines used in baseline or chain (continue) dimensions. It sets the distance that one dimension is above the other.

Color (DIMCLRD)
You can change the color of dimension lines so that they appear different than the other dimension components.

Extension Line

Suppress 1st and 2nd (DIMSE1, DIMSE2)
As with dimension lines, you can suppress the generation of extension lines. This can be useful when you have overlapping extension lines or an extension line would overlap an object or a center line.

Extension (DIMEXE)
This value is used to control how far the extension line extends past the dimension line.

Origin Offset (DIMEXO)
This value sets the distance that the extension lines start away from the pick points. It creates the extension gap between the extension line and the object being dimensioned.

Color (DIMCLRE)
As with dimension lines, you can change the color of extension lines.

Arrowheads

This area controls the termination symbols that are placed on the ends of extension or leader lines. AutoCAD refers to the termination symbols as arrowheads even though you can have symbols other than an arrow.

Icon Boxes
Picking on the icon boxes lets you cycle through the different arrowhead types.

1st and 2nd (DIMBLK1, DIMBLK2)
This is a pop-up list that allows you to select independently the names of the arrowhead types. Refer to Figure 6.11 for the pop-up list. The 1st and 2nd arrowheads can use different blocks simply by setting the 1st and then the 2nd arrowheads in that order. This is controlled by the DIMSAH dimension variable.

Size (DIMASZ)
Here you set the size of the arrowhead. Remember that the final size of the arrowheads on your drawing is governed by this size multiplied by the Overall Scale factor.

Figure 6.11
Different arrowhead styles

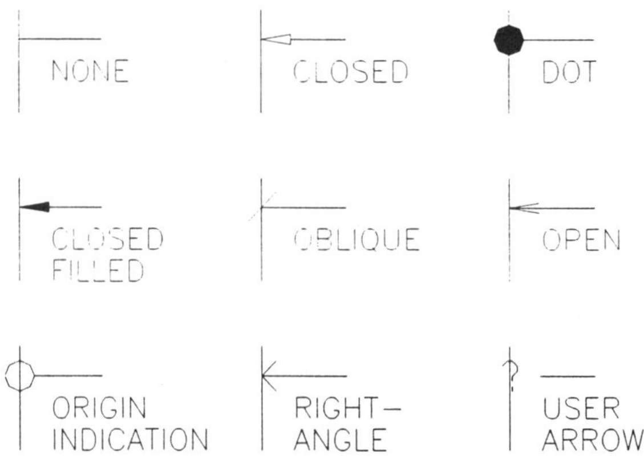

Center

Mark (DIMCEN positive value)
This button is used to place a marker in the center of arcs or circles when using radius, diameter, or center commands.

Line (DIMCEN negative value)
This button is used when you desire center lines as well as center marks when dimensioning arcs or circles.

None (DIMCEN zero)
This button is used when you do not want any mark when dimensioning arcs or circles.

Size (DIMCEN)
This controls the size of the mark and extension of the lines beyond the circle or arc.

Scale

Overall Scale (DIMSCALE)
The value in the Overall Scale box is a factor that is applied to all the size settings that control the appearance of the dimension components. A factor of 1 has no effect; greater that 1 increases the size, less than 1 reduces it. This does not change the values entered in the settings but it does multiply them to arrive at the displayed dimension components. A practical use of Feature Scaling is to enter the desired plot scale as the factor. An example would be 1/4"=1'-0" or 1:48; 48 is the scale factor. The dimension components would then be multiplied by 48 so that they would be

the correct size when plotted.

Scale to Paper Space (DIMSCALE zero)
The Scale to Paper Space box is used when the paper space environment is being used. When activated, AutoCAD grays over the Overall Scale box and computes the scale factor based on the scaling between the current model space viewport and paper space. This sets the DIMSCALE variable to 0.0.

Format Dialog Box

The Format dialog box, under the Dimension Styles dialog box, controls the position of the text in the dimension. Refer to Figure 6.12.

Figure 6.12
Format dialog box

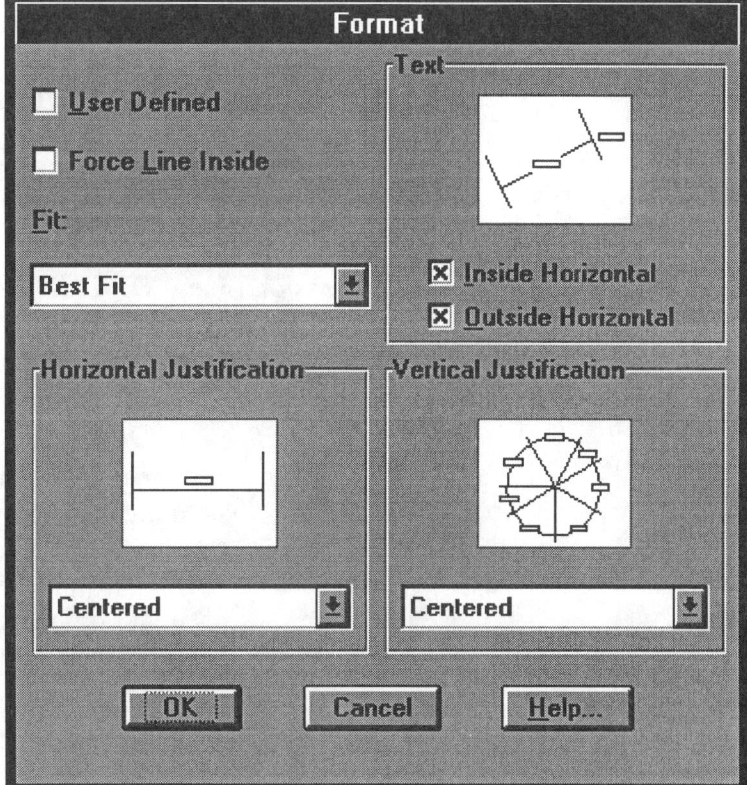

The following is a description of the various areas in the Format dialog box.

User Defined (DIMUPT)
This box, when checked, allows the user to drag the dimension text along the dimension line when placing the dimensions on the object.

Force Line Inside (DIMTOFL)
This setting forces dimension lines to be drawn inside the extension

lines regardless of the placement of the text.

Fit (DIMFIT)
This pop-up list controls how the text and the arrows behave. The
following is a list of the different positions:

Text and Arrows	DIMFIT = 0
Text Only	DIMFIT = 1
Arrows Only	DIMFIT = 2
Best Fit	DIMFIT = 3
Leader	DIMFIT = 4

Text (DIMTIH, DIMTOH)
These boxes control whether the text will be horizontal regardless
of the dimension line orientation (mechanical style) or, if turned off,
aligned to the dimension line (architectural style).

Horizontal Justification (DIMJUST)
A pop-up list is used to set horizontal placement of dimension text.
The following is a list of the different justifications:

Centered	DIMJUST = 0
1st Extension Line	DIMJUST = 1
2nd Extension Line	DIMJUST = 2
Over 1st Extension	DIMJUST = 3
Over 2nd Extension	DIMJUST = 4

Vertical Justification (DIMTAD)
A pop-up list is used to set vertical placement of dimension text.

Centered	The dimension line is split and the text is centered in the opening. DIMTAD = 0.
Above	The dimension line remains solid and the text is placed above the line by a distance linked to the value of the text height. DIMTAD = 1.
Outside	This setting places the text outside the extension lines. DIMTAD = 2.

Annotation Dialog Box
This dialog box, which is under the Dimension Styles dialog box, controls
the appearance of the text. Refer to Figure 6.13.

The following is a description of the areas in the Annotation dialog box.

Primary Units
Units (DIMUNIT)
This button displays another subdialog box called Primary Units.
Refer to Figure 6.14. The Units button is used to set the unit format
in which you will dimension, such as decimal or architectural. The

precision button is used to set the precision of the displayed dimension.

Prefix
This allows the addition of a prefix to a dimension.

Suffix
This allows the addition of a suffix to a dimension.

Icon Box (below the Suffix Box)
This box displays the current appearance of the text in regard to the use of tolerances. Each time you pick on the icon box, it displays the next tolerance type in sequence.

Figure 6.13
Annotation subdialog box

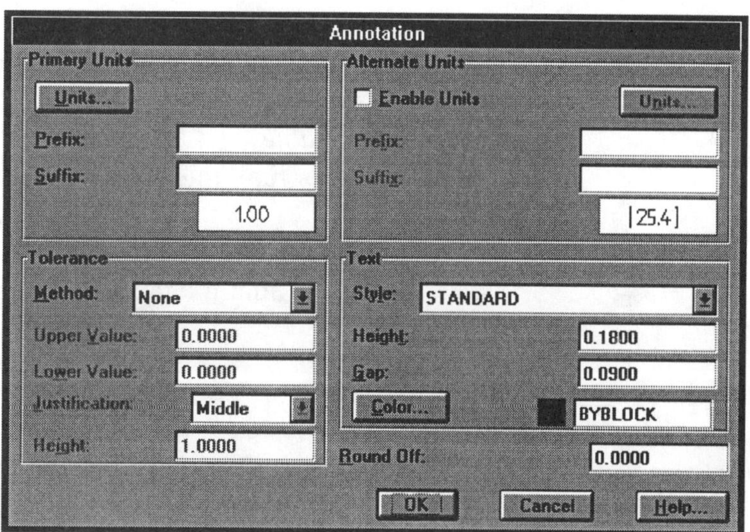

Figure 6.14
Primary Units subdialog box

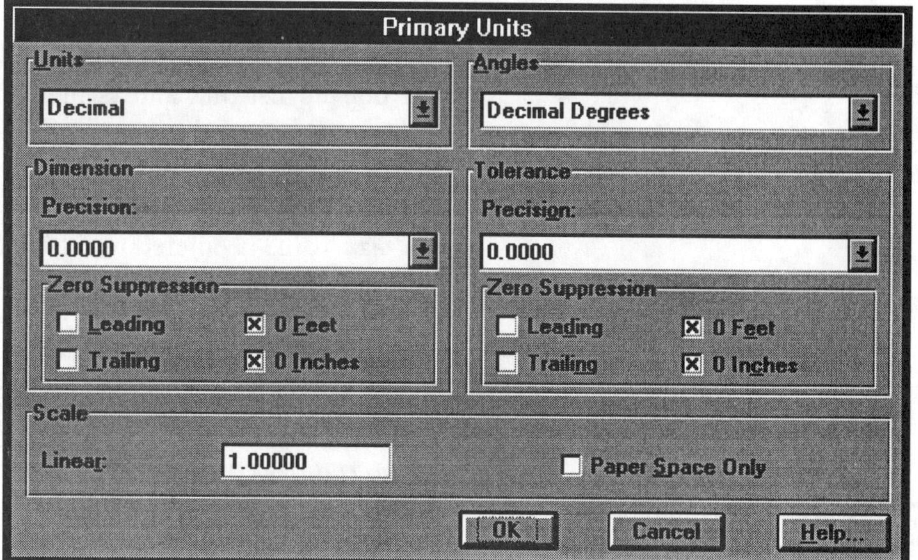

Alternate Units

This area allows the addition of alternate units as well as the primary units. This is commonly used when dual-dimensioning is required. Refer to Figure 6.13.

Enable Units
Allows alternate units.

Units, Prefix, Suffix
The settings for alternate units.

Tolerance

This area is used to add machining tolerances to dimensions.

Method
A pop-up list to identify the method of tolerancing.

Upper Value
The upper limit tolerance value.

Lower Value
The lower limit tolerance value

Justification
The position of the tolerance text

Height
A size value is entered to set the text height used for tolerance values when activated.

Text

Style (DIMTXSTY)
A pop-up list that allows the choice of text style from a list of previously created text styles.

Height (DIMTXT)
A size value is entered to set the text height used for dimensions. However, if the current text style already has a set text height, that height will be used instead of the dimension text height. NOTE: The final text height is arrived at by taking the DIMTXT height and multiplying it by the DIMSCALE factor.

Gap (DIMGAP)
This setting is used to control the amount of space between the dimension text and the dimension line. It also is used to draw a box around the text dimension, indicating a reference value. If you set

the DIMGAP variable to a negative value, a box is drawn around the text. You cannot enter a negative value in the dialog box; it must be done from the command line. The "Basic" tolerance method dialog box setting changes the DIMGAP value to a negative.

Color (DIMCLRT)
Controls the color of the dimension text.

Round Off (DIMRND)

This value is used to determine the smallest value that can be displayed in the dimension text. It is similar to the precision factor in the Units dialog box. You decide what the smallest value will be. For example, if you set it to 1, only integers will be displayed.

6.7 Geometric Tolerancing

Perfectly regular shapes or exact locations are not possible within our current means of manufacturing production. Because of this, some allowable variation in the shape or location must be permitted. These variances are referred to as tolerances, or because we are dealing with geometric shapes, geometric tolerances. To simplify the specification of geometric tolerances, the ANSI Y14.5 Dimensioning and Tolerancing Standard identifies standard symbols for shape and location tolerances. Refer to Figure 6.15 for illustrations of these symbols. The geometric tolerance symbols and values are placed within frames, or enclosed boxes. These frames are placed together to form a combined frame describing the entire tolerance characteristic. Refer to the typical symbol application at the bottom of Figure 6.15 for a representation of a single frame (datum identifier) and a combined frame (geometric symbol + diameter modifier + tolerance + datum).

AutoCAD Geometric Symbol Dialog Box

AutoCAD has incorporated the standard geometric symbols into its program with a geometric tolerancing dialog box accessed through the TOLERANCE command. Refer to Figure 6.16. You can select any of the depicted symbols or choose the last one, which is blank. When you pick one of the symbols or the blank, you are presented with the Geometric Tolerance dialog box.

Geometric Tolerance Dialog Box

Use this dialog box to piece together various components to make a frame. Refer to Figure 6.17.

The symbol shown in this area depends on the symbol picked in the symbol box. In Figure 6.16, the concentricity symbol was picked. The symbol will be enclosed in a box and added to the beginning of the tolerance frame. Note: If no symbol was picked, then no box will be added to the front.

Figure 6.15
Geometric tolerance symbol definitions

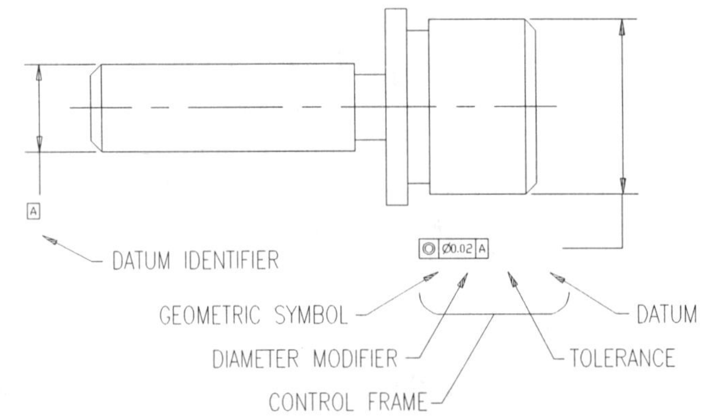

Figure 6.16
Symbol (Geometric) dialog box

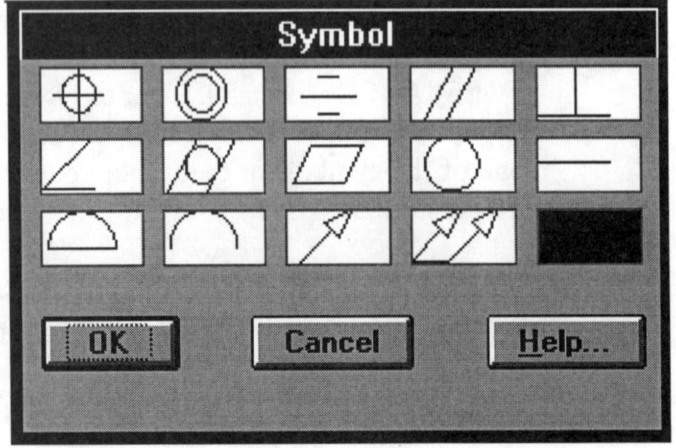

Tolerance 1 and 2 Area

This area creates the tolerance value box. If you pick the space before the tolerance value, you can add the diameter symbol shown in Figure 6.17. If you pick the space after the tolerance value, you are presented with a dialog box as shown in Figure 6.18. Use this box to add a material modifier after the tolerance value.

Datum 1, 2, and 3 Area

This area creates the datum reference letter as shown in Figure 6.17. You can also add a material modifier following it.

Height Area

This area creates a projected tolerance zone value. If you pick in the space following that value, you can add a projected zone symbol, which is a P enclosed in circle.

Datum Identifier

This area creates a datum identifier. It is usually a letter, preceded and followed by a dash, as in -A-. This area is usually used by itself to place a datum identifier on the drawing. Refer to Figure 6.15 for a typical symbol application.

Once you have used the dialog box to piece together the components that will make up the frame, and have pressed OK, AutoCAD will ask you to position the frame and will draw it in for you. Refer to the typical symbol application shown at the bottom of Figure 6.15.

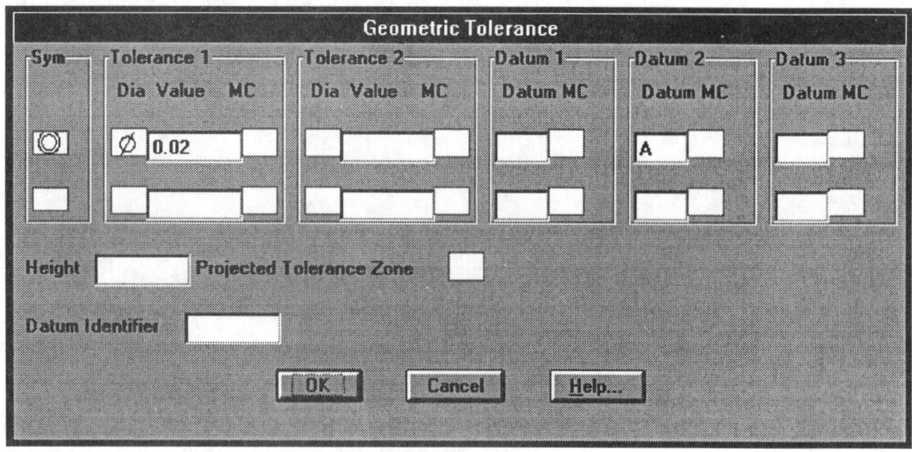

Figure 6.17
Geometric Tolerance dialog box

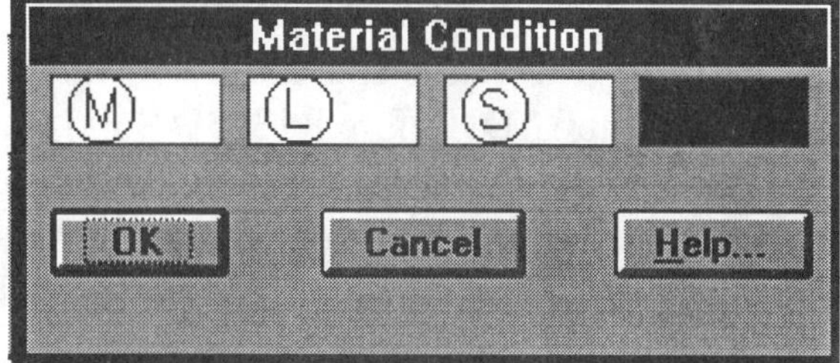

Figure 6.18
Material Condition dialog box

3D Modeling

7.1 Introduction

This chapter will review the aspects of 3D modeling involving 3-dimensional creation and rendering. The previous methods will be reviewed while the new additions will be explained in more detail with emphasis on the integrated 3D Solid Modeling and the new Rendering capabilities for those new to 3D Solid Modeling and Rendering. It is important to note that, because integrated solid modeling was not available to AutoCAD users before R13, there may be many who have never been exposed to it before. For those in this position, a brief but comprehensive exploration can be found in the pages ahead.

7.2 Old and New

The techniques for moving around and creating in 3D space have not changed drastically from R12 to R13. You still make use of the UCS (User Coordinate System) to establish working planes. The VPOINT command is still used to generate axonometric views of your 3D model, while DVIEW will help create perspective views. The standard surface commands, such as 3DFACE or REVSURF, work as they did before, creating single or multiple (mesh) surfaces, and the primitive surface objects such as box and sphere are available but require the AI_ prefix to create them, such as AI_SPHERE.

What has changed is the integration of 3D Solid Modeling directly into AutoCAD. Before R13, 3D Solid Modeling was achieved through the use of the Advance Modeling Extension (AME). This was an add-on application program that was purchased separately and loaded whenever you required solid modeling. Now 3D solids are native primitives, just like circles and lines, and can be modified to a certain extent like those 2-

dimensional primitives. When you enter BOX on the command line, you will now be creating a 3 dimensional solid box object.

The other major change to 3D modeling has been the enhancement of the rendering capabilities. The RENDER utility has been upgraded to include new rendering modes, such as Gouraud and Phong. The Surface Finish properties have been replaced with Material properties giving more control as well as making the transition to Autodesk's AutoVision easier. In the Windows version, you can save rendered images in the BMP format.

7.3 Introduction to Integrated Solid Modeling

Solid modeling creates 3-dimensional models with database properties, giving the models mass and density. The computer "believes" the model is a solid form, from the outside through to its inner core (refer to Figure 7.1), so capabilities that are unavailable with wireframe or surfaced modeling can be accessed with solid modeling. Think of yourself as a sculptor or a modeler of clay when you approach solid modeling. You start with a solid block, carve away a piece here, bore a hole there, or add a protrusion. This is how solid modeling works - by addition and subtraction. That is the basic process that you, as the user, need to understand. However, in the background, complex mathematical operations are taking place to accomplish the seemingly simple additions and subtractions. As more and more of these subtractions and additions are made, the mathematical intricacies and convolutions increase. And that means, of course, there is a price to pay. But the benefits in the model definition - especially in prototype generation and modification - can outweigh the disadvantage of extra calculation time.

Figure 7.1
Solid model of an apple

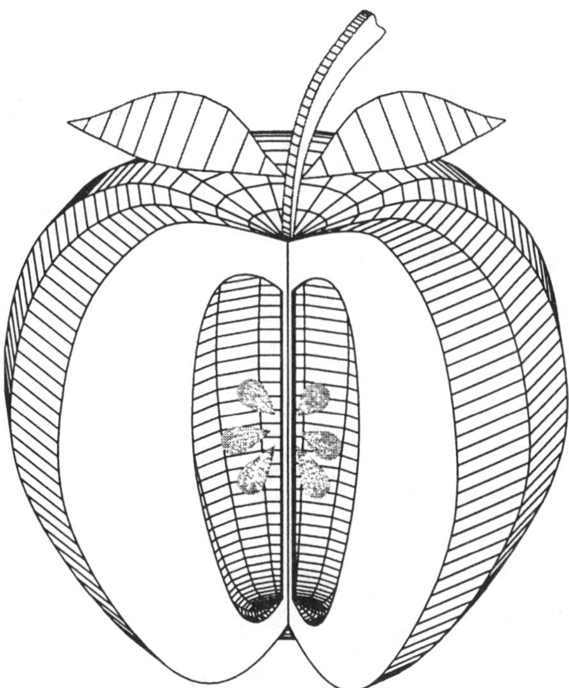

It is important to note that the benefits of wireframe and surfaced modeling are not lost by adding solid modeling. Each method has its own place. There are, in fact, many situations in which solid modeling does not perform well, such as in terrain modeling. Solid modeling was not intended for that application; it is much more useful in the design of a mechanical component.

In addition, the techniques of model creation mastered up to this point were not learned in vain. They will remain as important in the creation of solid models as they were in the creation of wireframe and surfaced models. Solid modeling complements, rather than usurps, the other modeling methods. After some exploration of its techniques, you will soon locate the niche in which to place it.

7.4 Advanced Modeling Extension

Before Release 13, AutoCAD made use of an extension program to create solid models; this was referred to as Advanced Modeling Extension or AME. Entities created with AME were AME blocks. Solid modeling has now been totally integrated into the AutoCAD program and the entities created are now referred to as 3D solids. AME solids and 3D solids are totally different entities. Because of this, you must convert AME solids from previous releases to 3D solids. This can be accomplished with the AMECONVERT command. Because the new 3D solids are more accurate than the previous AME solids, you may see some differences in the converted AME model.

7.5 Solids and Regions

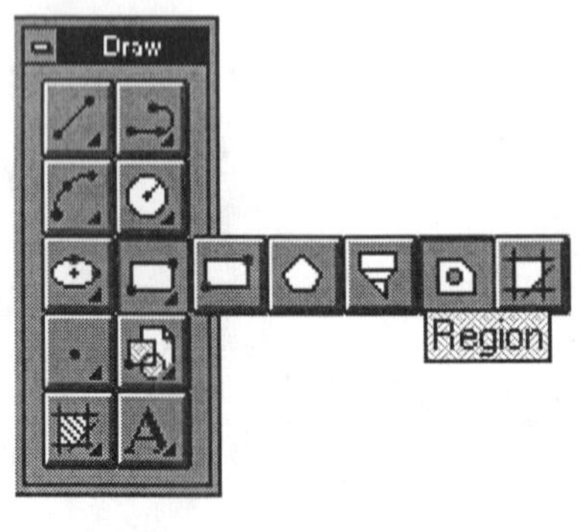

There are two types of entities that make use of solid modeling commands - 3D solids and regions. 3D solids are 3-dimensional objects that have solid properties. Regions can be thought of as flat solids (refer to Figure 7.2); they have physical and material properties, but they have no thickness and are 2-dimensional.

Figure 7.2
A region

Complex 3D solids and regions can be created using the same commands, except that solids use 3-dimensional primitives, such as boxes and cylinders, and regions use 2-dimensional primitives, such as circles and polygons. Regions are composed of totally enclosed areas called loops. Loops can be combinations of lines, polylines, circles, arcs, ellipses, elliptical arcs, splines, 3D faces, traces, and solids (2D). These entities must form closed loops and be planar (on a flat plane) in nature. To turn the basic entities into a region, use the REGION command. Once you have created region loops, you can make use of the solid modeling commands such as UNION or SUBTRACT to make more complex regions or use the EXTRUDE command to generate complex profiled 3D solids. In either case, you can use the MASSPROP command to extract information such as the calculated area and the perimeter of the region.

It should be noted that, even though the same commands are used to form the complex shapes, 3D solids and regions cannot be combined. Because 3D solids are 3-dimensional and regions are 2-dimensional, 3D solids can combine with 3D solids and regions with regions but there can never be a mix of the two. However, a region can be made 3-dimensional, and a 3D solid 2-dimensional, using a process that will be explained later.

Note: For the sake of simplicity, and because solids and regions use similar techniques for creation, the discussion here will focus on 3D solids.

Construction and Display of 3D Solids

The primitives used by Solid Modeling to create final, complex forms can be viewed as building blocks, added to or subtracted from each other to create the final form. (Note: 3D solids also can be created by extruding revolving 2D objects.) The building blocks for 3D solids are boxes, wedges, cylinders, spheres, cones, and tori. Solid modeling can create these basic forms.

Once created, primitives can be combined in a number of ways to form what is called a composite model. A composite model is the final desired result of any combination of primitives or other composites. There are two types of composite models: composite 3D solids and composite regions. As is true of primitive 3D solids and regions, composite 3D solids and regions cannot be combined.

The composite model can be enhanced by special editing. Chamfering, filleting, slicing, and sectioning are types of 3D solid editing.

Like surface models, 3D solids can be displayed in four ways: wireframe, hidden line removed, shaded, and rendered. To control the display, 3D solids have some system variables that are particular to them. 3D solids also can provide graphic information to aid in the creation of 2-dimensional drafting drawings. These capabilities will be explained in greater detail later.

Solid modeling keeps track of the material properties of 3D solids for use within AutoCAD in mass property calculations or outside AutoCAD for finite element analysis.

7.6 Primitive Creation

Six commands will create the six basic 3D solid primitives: BOX, WEDGE, CYLINDER, CONE, SPHERE, and TORUS. These commands have different options, to be used according to the primitive being created. However, their similarities allow for easy mastery. These primitives are very similar to the surfaced primitives. Figure 7.3 illustrates their various forms. The following explains each primitive creation command and its options.

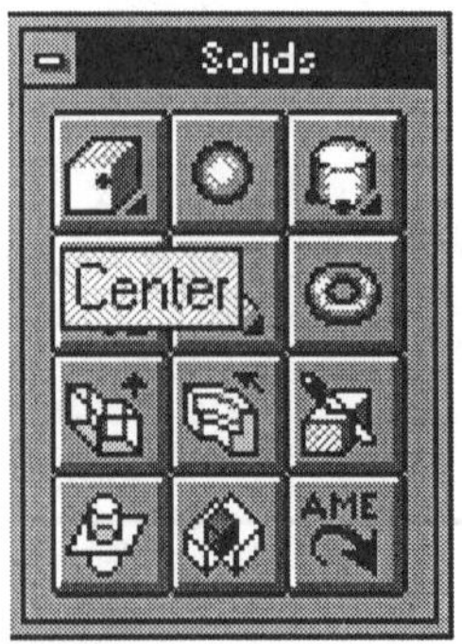

BOX   Creates a 3D solid box by defining its diagonal corners, by defining its base and height, or by indicating its center and overall dimensions. A rubberband technique is used to visually determine sizes. It has two options. The Center option allows the user to define the center of the box. The Corner of Box option allows the user to define the corners of the box.

WEDGE   Creates a 3D solid wedge. Its parameters are identical to that of the BOX command. The base is parallel to the current working plane and the sloped face tapers along the X axis.

Figure 7.3
Primitive 3D solids

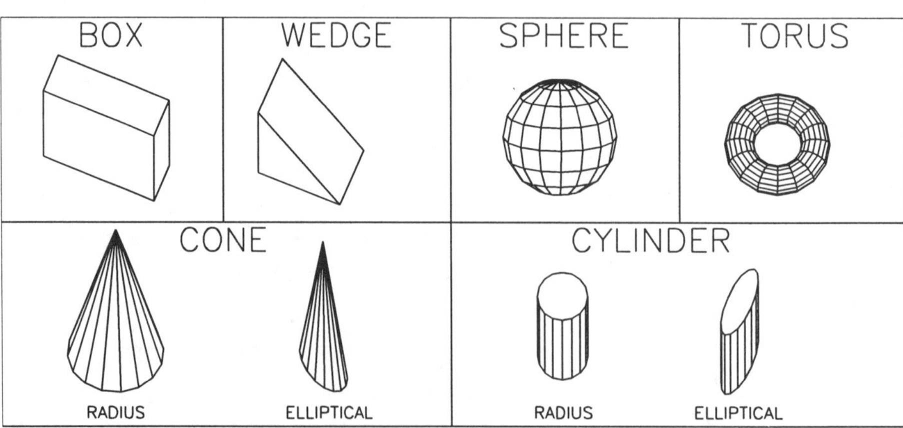

CYLINDER   Creates a 3D solid cylinder by defining its base and height. CYLINDER has two options. The Elliptical option allows the user to define the axis of the ellipse. The Center Point option allows the user to define the center of the cylinder.

CONE   Creates a 3D solid cone. Its parameters are identical to that of the CYLINDER command, except for references to the apex of the cone.

SPHERE   Creates a 3D solid sphere by defining its radius or diameter and its center.

TORUS   Creates a 3D solid torus, which is a donut shape, by defining two radii: one for the tube shape and one from the center of the torus to the center of the tube. If the radius of the tube is greater that the torus radius, a self-intersecting torus, resembling a football in shape, is formed.

Primitives from 2D Entities

There are two commands that will create 3D solid primitives from 2-dimensional entities or regions: EXTRUDE and REVOLVE. The primitive 3D solids created by these commands are shown in Figure 7.4. The following explains each command.

Figure 7.4
Primitive 3D solids from 2D objects

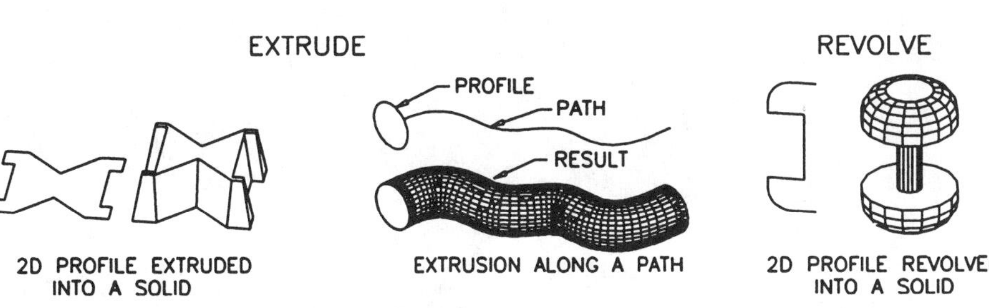

The EXTRUDE Command

The EXTRUDE command creates a 3D solid by extruding existing 2-dimensional entities or regions. You can select multiple objects on which to perform the extrusion. The extrusion always takes place perpendicular to the base of the entity, and it can have parallel or tapered sides. If you wish to create a sloped extrusion, base the taper on the angle measured in from the perpendicular sides of the extrusion. It must be greater than 0 and less than 90 degrees. It is also possible to extrude a profile along a 2D polyline path simply by picking the profile and the path.

The REVOLVE Command

The REVOLVE command creates a 3D solid by revolving a profile around an axis. This command is similar to the AutoCAD surface command REVSURF. Only one profile can be selected at a time, and only circles, polylines, polygons, ellipses, and region entities can be revolved. Blocks or 3D entities cannot be revolved.

7.7 Composite Solids and Relation Commands

A complex form, known as a composite, is created through the interrelationship of two primitives (solids with solids or regions with regions). Once the relationship is determined, a composite is formed. The process is very simple.

For example, to insert a hole through a rectangular plate, where the plate is a box solid, and the hole is a cylinder solid, identify the relationship between the box and the cylinder by subtracting the volume of the cylinder from the volume of the box. The final result is a plate with a hole through it, or a composite. See Figure 7.5.

Figure 7.5
Creating a hole in a solid plate

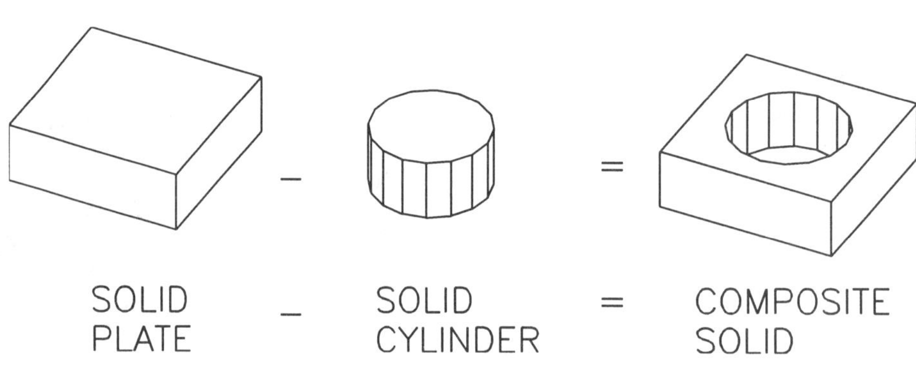

Relation Commands

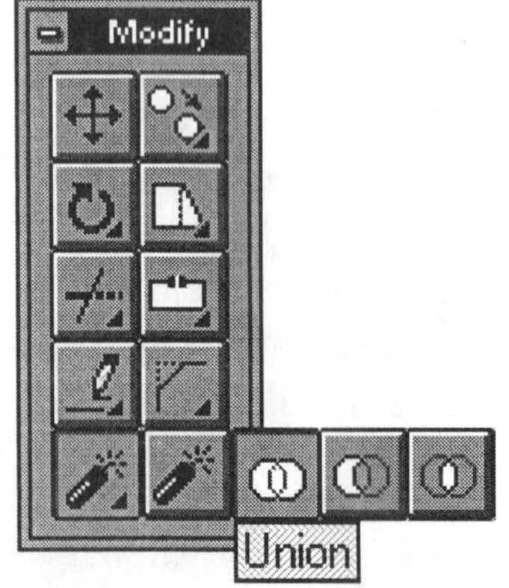

There are three commands to relate primitives to each other: UNION, SUBTRACT, and INTERSECT. UNION is used to add solids to each other, SUBTRACT is used to subtract solids from one another, and INTERSECT is used to create a composite from the intersection of two solids. Figure 7.6 illustrates the relationships between solids created by these three commands. You can repeat the relationship commands with any two solids, composite or primitive, to create as complex a solid object as desired. The tools for relating solids can be found under the Explode flyout of the Modify toolbar.

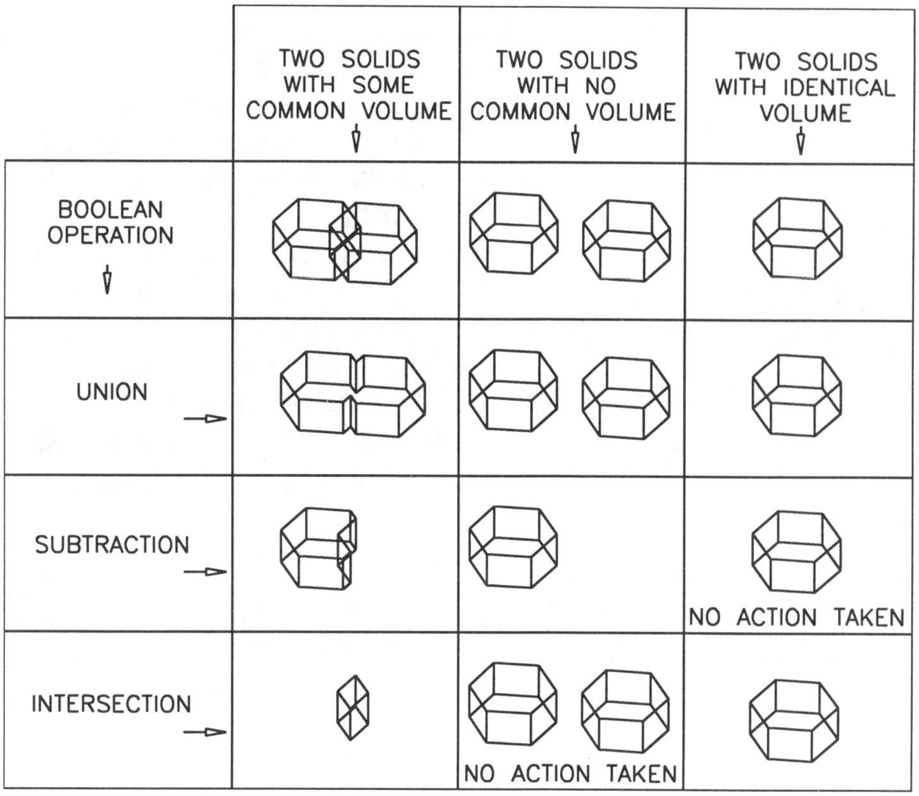

Figure 7.6
Relationships between solids

7.8 Modifying Composites

To further enhance your composite model, use the standard modify commands - CHAMFER and FILLET and the 3D solid command SLICE. Because you are modifying 3-dimensional solids, the CHAMFER and FILLET commands behave slightly differently than they do when used on 2-dimensional entities. The following is an explanation of the three commands.

The CHAMFER Command

To produce a chamfer of a solid, use the CHAMFER command. It will automatically subtract the solid area defined by the CHAMFER settings. To use the command, refer to Figure 7.7 and follow this procedure.

Command: **CHAMFER**
(TRIM mode) Current chamfer Dist1 = 0   Dist2 = 0 Polylines/ Distance/ Angle/ Trim/ Method/ <Select first line>: **pick edge to be**

chamfered

Select base surface: **select the base surface from which to start the chamfer**

Next/<OK>: **one of the two surfaces adjoining the selected edge is highlighted; either OK it to be used as the base surface or use the Next option to move to the next surface**

Enter base surface distance: **enter the distance in from the edge of the base surface that will represent the first edge of the chamfer**

Enter other surface distance: **enter the second distance along the adjacent surface**

Loop/<select edge>: **pick as many edges that surround (are adjacent to) the base surface**

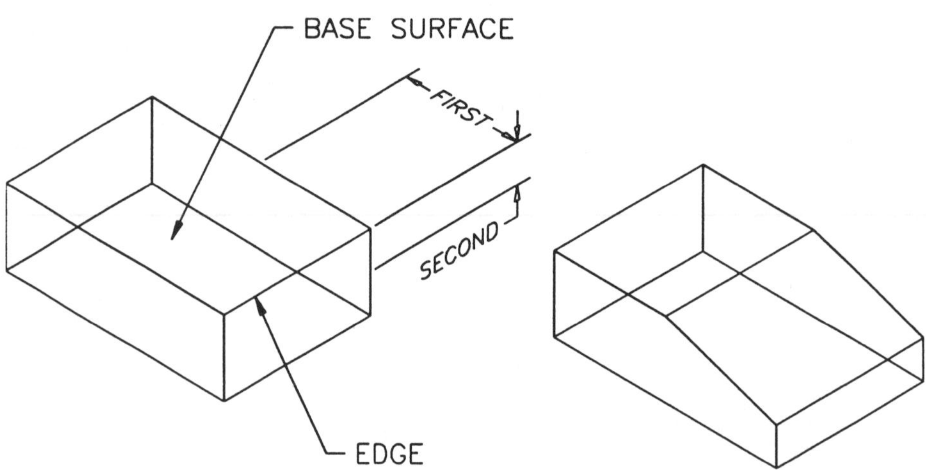

Figure 7.7
The CHAMFER command

The FILLET Command

To create a fillet along the edge of a solid, use the FILLET command. It creates an internal or external arc (concave or convex) along selected edges of a solid. Refer to Figure 7.8. The procedure to use the FILLET command follows.

Command: **FILLET**

(TRIM mode) Current fillet radius = 0 Polyline/Radius/Trim/<Select first object>: **pick an edge of the solid to fillet**

Enter radius <0>: **enter the desired radius of the fillet**

Chain/Radius/<Select edge>:   **pick the edges to be filleted**

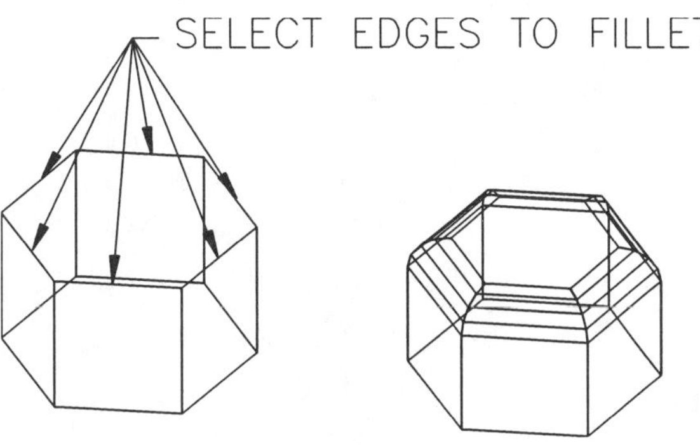

Figure 7.8
The FILLET command

Slicing a Solid in Two

AutoCAD has the ability to take a solid and slice it into two pieces along a user-defined plane. This ability is accessed with the SLICE command. Once the slice has been made, both new solids or only one may be retained. The options for defining the slicing plane are Object, Zaxis, View, XY, YZ, ZX, and 3Points. Refer to Figure 7.9 and the following procedure.

Command: **SLICE**
Select objects: **pick the solid to be sliced**
Slicing plane by Object/Zaxis/View/XY/YZ/ZX/<3 points>: **enter the desired method for specifying the slicing plane**
Both sides/<Point on the desired side of the plane: **press enter to identify the desired side to retain or enter Both to keep both sides**

Figure 7.9
The SLICE command

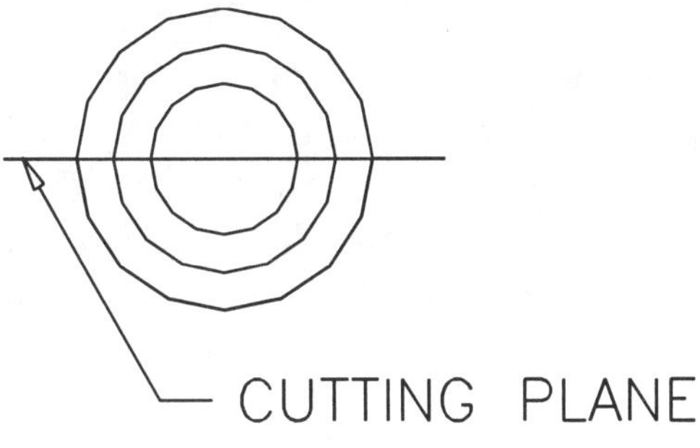

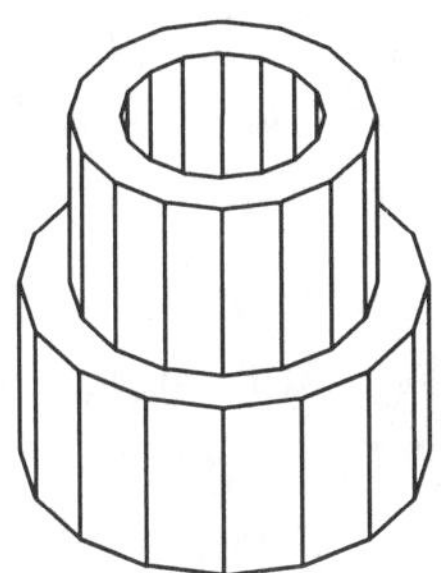

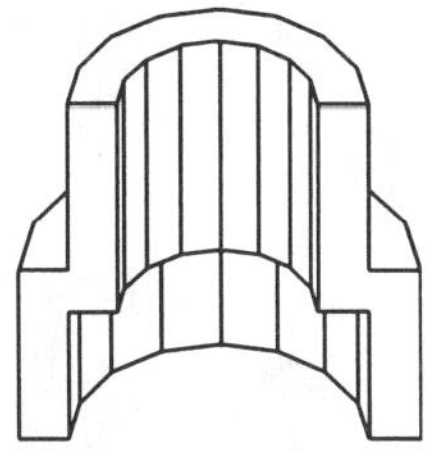

The following are descriptions of the slicing plane options.

Object   Aligns the slicing plane with an object such as a circle, ellipse, circular or elliptical arc, 2D spline, or 2D polyline segment.

Zaxis   Defines the slicing plane by a specified point on the Z axis of the XY plane.

View   Aligns the slicing plane with the current viewport's viewing plane.

XY   Aligns the slicing plane with the current UCS XY plane.

YZ   Aligns the slicing plane with the current UCS YZ plane.

ZX   Aligns the slicing plane with the current UCS ZX plane.

3Points   Defines the slicing plane by identifying 3 points on the plane.

7.9 3D Solids Representation

A solid model can be displayed as wireframe, hidden line removed, shaded, and rendered. However, there are two variables that have a direct effect on those types of displays. These variables are ISOLINES and FACETRES. The ISOLINES variable controls the number of tessellation lines that are used to define the curved features of the model in wireframe. Tessellation lines are the parallel lines used to define the curve of a surface for easier visualization. The FACETRES variable controls the resolution of the facets that are created when you perform a hidden line-removal, shaded, or rendered display of a solid. You may enter an integer value from 0 to 2047 for the number of isolines per surface of a solid. The higher the value, the greater the number of isolines. You may enter a value from 0.01 to 10.0 for the facet resolution. The higher the value, the more facets that are created and the smoother the resultant figure.

The Effect of ISOLINES and FACETRES Settings on a Sphere

Look at the sphere shown in Figure 7.10, part A. This sphere was created with an ISOLINES value of 5. Only a few lines are used to define the curved surfaces. Now refer to parts B, C, and D of Figure 7.10. The sphere in Part B is shown on wireframe with an ISOLINES setting of 15. Because of the higher number, more isolines are drawn, giving a clearer view of the sphere. However, it takes longer to manipulate the view of the model with a higher ISOLINES setting. Finally, refer to the last two spheres, hidden lined removed and with FACETRES settings of .25 and .5. You can see that the ISOLINES and FACETRES variables are independent of each other. You can change the ISOLINES and FACETRES variables at any time to increase or decrease the number of lines and facets when representing the solid model. Use the least number of isolines that you can and still be able to manipulate the solid. Use the least number of facets possible when creating initial settings for rendering and then increase the number for the final render.

Figure 7.10
Wireframe and hidden displays

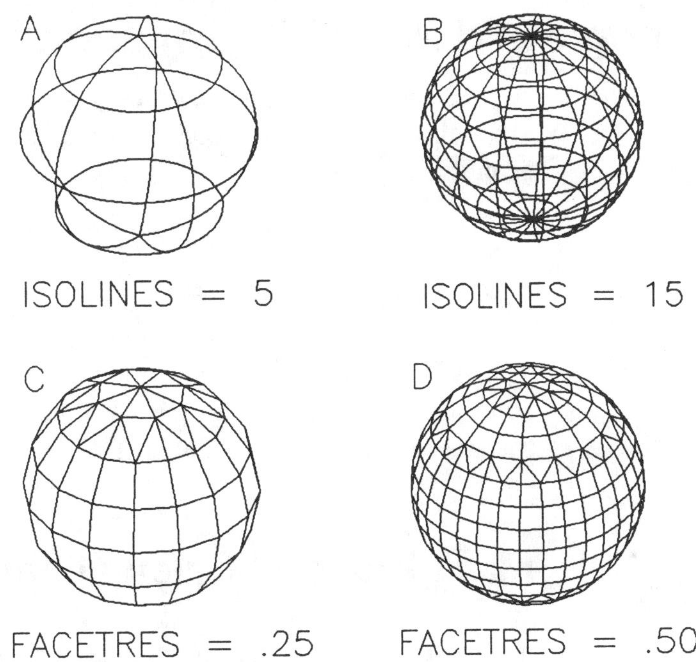

2D Representation of A Solid

Only one command is used to create a 2 dimensional representation of a solid. The SECTION command will create a section view automatically by specifying the cutting plane. It works very much like the SLICE command. But instead of slicing the model, it creates a profile outline of the cut area. Refer to Figure 7.11 and the following procedure.

Command: **SECTION**

Select objects: **pick the solid to be sectioned**
Slicing plane by Object/Zaxis/View/XY/YZ/ZX/<3 points>: **enter the
   desired method for specifying the sectioning plane**

Figure 7.11
Creating a section view

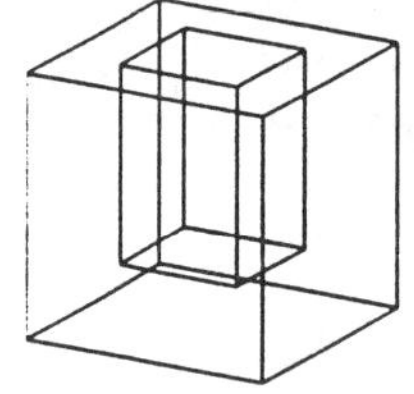
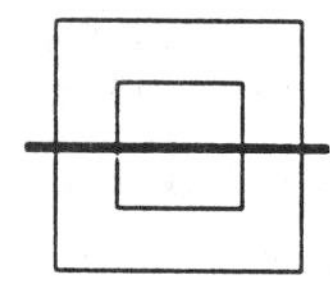
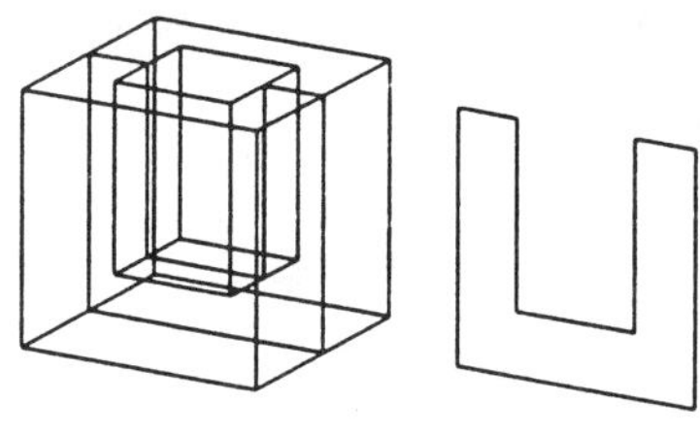

7.10 Extracting Solid Model Information

As with regular AutoCAD entities, you can inquire and receive information about the model you are constructing. You can inquire about area as well as mass properties.

Area Calculations

The AREA command displays the calculated surfaced areas of selected solids and regions. You can use the add option of the area command to total the areas of several individual solids.

Mass Property Calculations

You can extract mass properties from solids and regions. This is accomplished with the MASSPROP command by selecting the solid model from which you wish to extract the mass property information. Refer to the following data for the sample mass properties of a 2 inch cube.

```
------------------ SOLIDS ------------------------
Mass:                       8.0000
Volume:                     8.0000
Bounding box:      X:       0.0000 -- 2.0000
                   Y:       0.0000 -- 2.0000
                   Z:       0.0000 -- 2.0000
Centroid:          X:       1.0000
                   Y:       1.0000
                   Z:       1.0000
Moments of inertia: X:      21.3333
                    Y:      21.3333
                    Z:      21.3333
```

Products of inertia: XY: 8.0000
                      YZ: 8.0000
                      ZX: 8.0000
Radii of gyration: X: 1.6330
                      Y: 1.6330
                      Z: 1.6330
Principle moments and X-Y-Z directions about centroid:
                      I: 5.333 along [1.0000 0.0000 0.0000]
                      J: 5.333 along [0.0000 1.0000 0.0000]
                      K: 5.333 along [0.0000 0.0000 1.0000]

DEFINITIONS OF MASS PROPERTY TERMS

Here are brief definitions of the terms used for the solid modeling mass property calculations as given by AutoCAD.

Mass	The measure of inertia of a body. Because AutoCAD uses a density of one, mass and volume have the same value.
Volume	Amount of space occupied by the selected object.
Bounding box	A 2D or 3D rectangular box that encloses the object and upon which the calculations are performed.
Centroid	Center of the selected object.
Moments of inertia	Amount of force required to rotate the selected object about its various axes.
Products of inertia	Values used in determining the forces causing the motion of an object.
Radii of gyration	Radial distance from the point of rotation at which the total mass must be concentrated.
Principle moments	X-Y-Z directions about centroid values derived from products of inertia; the first value is the axis through which the moment of inertia is the highest, the second is the axis through which the moment of inertia is the lowest, and the third lies between the highest and the lowest.

Indication of Solid Interferences

It is possible to exhibit the interferences between solids with overlapping masses. The INTERFERE command finds the interference of two or more solids and highlights the pairs that interfere. You can turn the interference volume into a separate solid if you desire. The command allows you to create two selection sets and compare the first set to the second. However, if you only select the first set, the solids in that set will be compared to one another.

7.11 Rendering

For AutoCAD users, rendering presents a design in an artistic form, giving an image a more realistic appearance. In CAD, rendering is the process of taking an image made of lines and adding tones across the surfaces between those lines. The tones range from light to dark and may be in black and white or a combination of other colors. Refer to Figure 7.12 for a rendered image.

Performing renderings with 3-dimensional models is an art in and of itself. Producing photo-realistic images is a long process and can require access to expensive hardware. Here, you will be introduced to a range of possible rendering techniques. Even this small taste will let you see the possibilities.

Figure 7.12
A rendered image

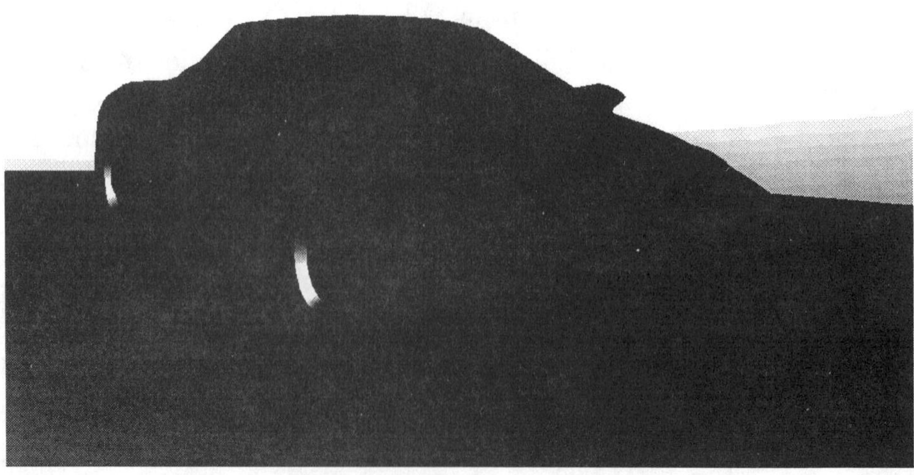

Render Procedure

To make rendering a relatively easy task, follow the procedure outlined next. This procedure identifies the major areas that will be explained in the text that follows.

1.   Open the desired model to be rendered.

2.   Load the RENDER utility. This is done automatically when the RENDER, LIGHT, RMAT, MATLIB, RPREF commands are used.

3.   Configure the RENDER utility to suit the computer's graphics. You are prompted automatically the first time the RENDER utility is used. To reconfigure, use the RCONFIG command.

4.   Create the desired pictorial views, axonometric or perspective. These should be stored under the VIEW command.

5.   Specify (place) the desired number and type of lights to illuminate the view using the LIGHT command. Although it is possible to create a rendering without specifying lights (AutoCAD would then use default settings to create the rendering), placing lights will give you more control over the final rendering.

6.   Load materials to be used in the drawing with the RMAT command. You will need to extract materials from a material library that can be accessed through the RMAT command or the MATLIB command.

7.   Assign material properties to objects, colors, or layers (to add highlights to the model) using the RMAT command.

8.   Assemble scenes that contain the desired view and lights utilizing the SCENE command.

9.   Set the rendering preferences, such as rendering type, smooth shading, and so on, using the RPREF command.

10.   Select the desired scene with the use of the RENDER command. The screen should display the model in the rendered form.

11.   Save the image on disk using the SAVEIMG command, so that it may be replayed at a later time.

12.   Replay an image using the REPLAY command.

The addition of lights varies the tone of the rendered images. When used in combination with materials, lights will also create highlights.

When lighting a scene, it is important to remember that the brightness of a surface is controlled by its relation to the light source. The closer the face is to being perpendicular to the source of light, the brighter the surface will be. Two other factors govern the brightness of a surface - reflection and roughness. These are controlled by the material property and will be discussed later.

There are four light types: ambient, distant, point, and spot. The ambient light is the background light. It creates illumination all around the model and is used to increase or decrease the overall brightness of all surfaces.

Distant light simulates a light source that is a great distance from the model, such as the sun. The casting of its light rays are parallel and its distance away from the model has no effect on the light. Only the direction it is pointing and its intensity affects the lighted model.

Point light radiates light from its source location, in an effect similar to that of a light bulb. The distance that the point light is away from the model affects the amount of light reaching the model. This phenomenon is referred to as fall-off and is controlled by using the inverse linear and inverse square options of the point light options. Light from point sources passes through surfaces and does not cast shadows. This type of light is useful for accenting an area or adding highlights. It can be used to simulate light bulbs placed in fixtures.

The spot light simulates the effects of spotlights to create brightly lit areas. If you have access to AutoVision, spotlights are also used to cast shadows. The spotlight's purpose is to generate a cone of light projecting from a source and falling on a particular area.

Placing the Lights

To make a model stand out, there must be a contrast between light and dark, controlled by the placement of lights.

When placing lights, direct at least one light diagonally upon the model from the left or right top of the screen. This produces a minimum of three tone levels.

If the model is large, such as a house, more lights may be needed in order to accent areas and increase the contrast between light and dark.

To add overall ambient light, use the LIGHT command and refer to the Ambient Light sliding bar on the Lights dialog box. Look at Figure 7.13. You can also change the color of the overall ambient light with the use of the color sliders bars in the ambient area.

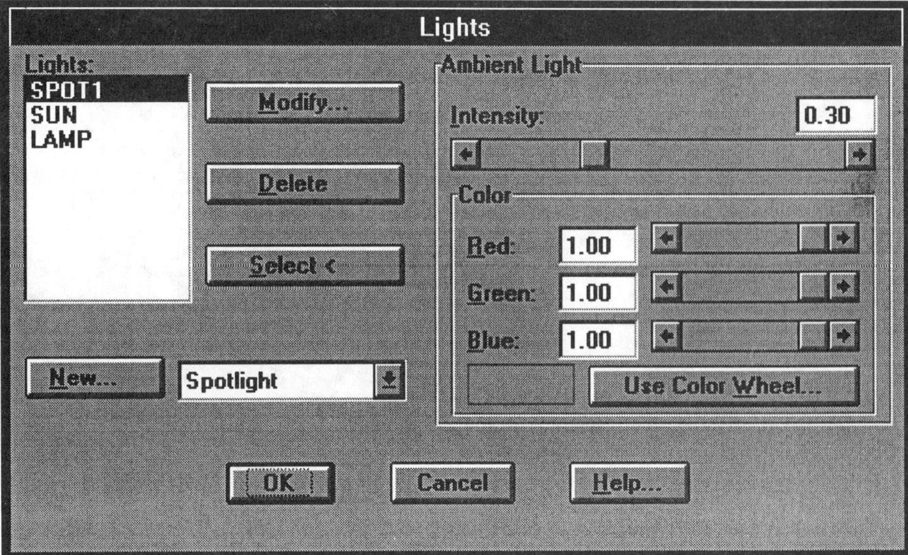

The procedure to place a new light is as follows:

1. Select NEW from the Lights dialog box.

2. Pick one of the three light types - point, distant, or spot. If you have AutoVision, then you can make use of the Spotlight option.

3   Now the New Light dialog box appears. Each light type has some common settings. At this point you give a name to the light. Each new light should have its own unique name. Also enter the Intensity. A value of 0 turns the light off. For point and spotlights, the value can be any real number. For distant lights, the value can be any real number between 0 and 1. The following are some unique settings for each light type.

POINT (refer to Figure 7.14)

The point light dialog box contains an Attenuation area. It controls the point light fall-off, the rate at which the point light intensity decreases as the distance from the light source increases. If you do not wish any decrease in light intensity, select the None box; if you want a gradual decrease in light intensity, select the Inverse linear box, and if you want a rapid decrease in light intensity with distance, select the Inverse square box. To place the point light, use the Modify button and to check its location, use the Show button.

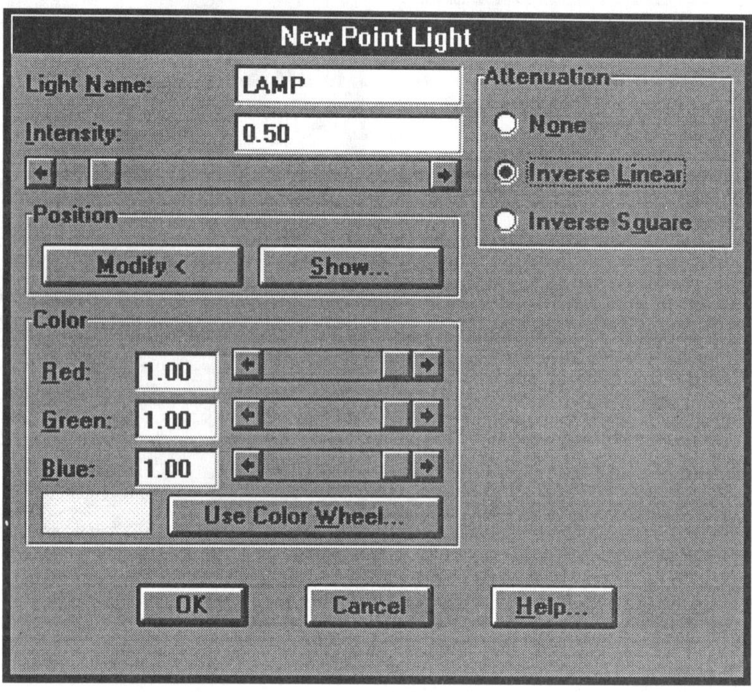

DISTANT (refer to Figure 7.15)

> The distant light is normally used to simulate the sun. To assist in its placement, you can use image boxes to define the Azimuth and Altitude. To identify the location the sun is shining toward, use the Modify button.

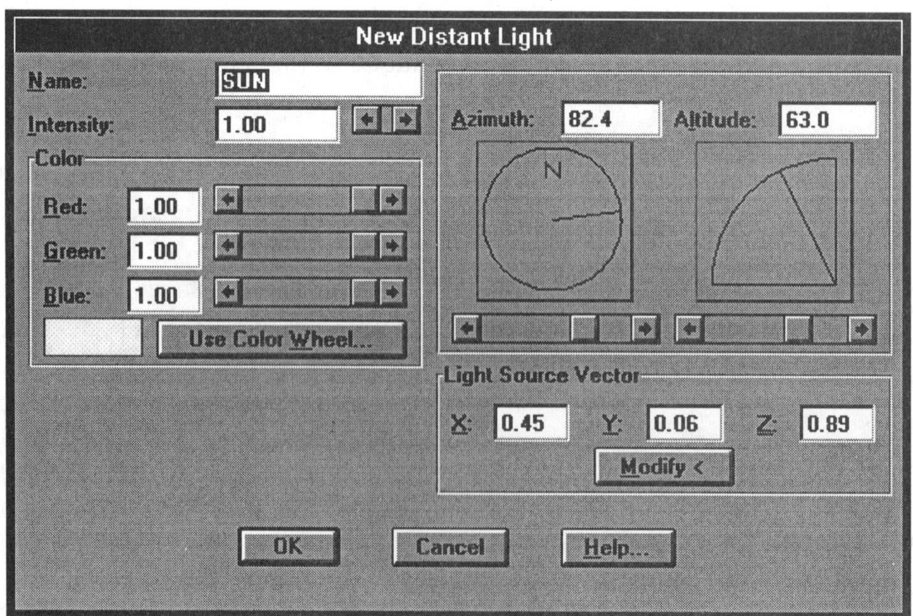

SPOTLIGHT (refer to Figure 7.16)

The spotlight is used to cast shadows. To define the area the light is falling upon, use the Hotspot and Falloff values. The Hotspot defines the area of the most definite shadow. The Falloff defines the area where the shadow gradually fades off. Like the point light, use the Modify and Show buttons to place the light. You will need to identify where the light is located and where it is pointing toward.

Figure 7.16
New Spotlight dialog box

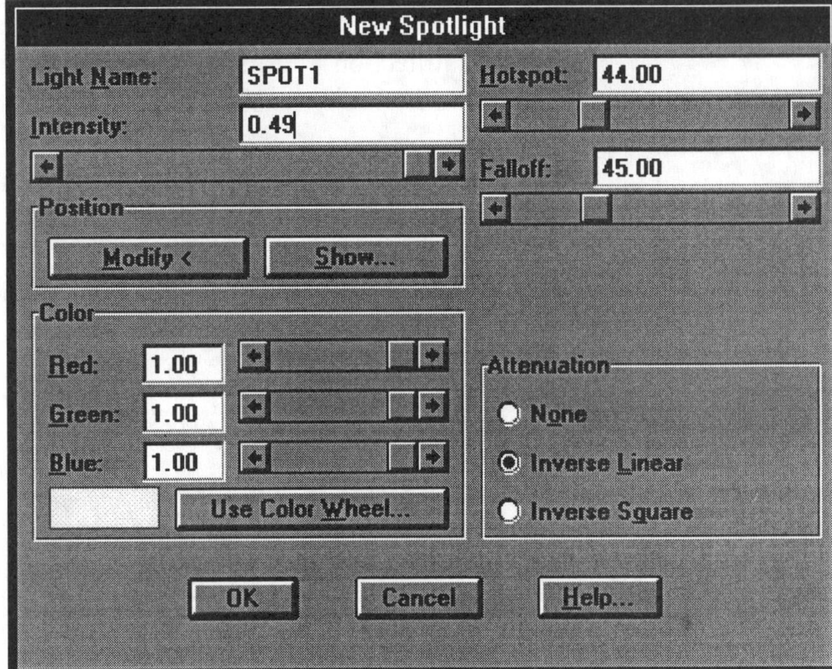

4. When you have accepted the light settings and placed the light, a block with the light's unique name appears at the given coordinate location. The size of the block is governed by the Icon Scale setting in the Rendering Preferences dialog box.

5. To modify a currently placed light, you can either pick the light name from the list or use the Select option to select the light block required from the Lights dialog box.

7.13 Material Properties

The Surface Finish properties of R12 have been replaced with the Material properties of R13. They are similar in some respects but Material properties give you more control and prepare you for using AutoVision materials.

Material properties control the way light is reflected from or absorbed by a surface. These properties can be attached to specific objects, specific colors, or layers. Refer to Figure 7.19. A material has four properties - color, ambient, reflection, and roughness; each property has an intensity value and a color. The intensity values can range from 0 to 1; the color is controlled by three slider bars. Refer to the following table for the properties and the effect of intensity values.

Material Properties	Setting = 0 (LOW)	Setting = 1 (HIGH)
ambient	dulls the finish color	brightens the finish color
reflection	makes surface light absorbing	makes surface highly reflective
roughness	provides small area of reflection	provides large area of reflection

You can enter any combination of values to generate individual materials. You can create your own materials or select pre-made materials from a material library.

Using Materials

The creation and attachment of materials is performed from the Materials dialog box. Refer to Figure 7.17.

Figure 7.17
Materials dialog box

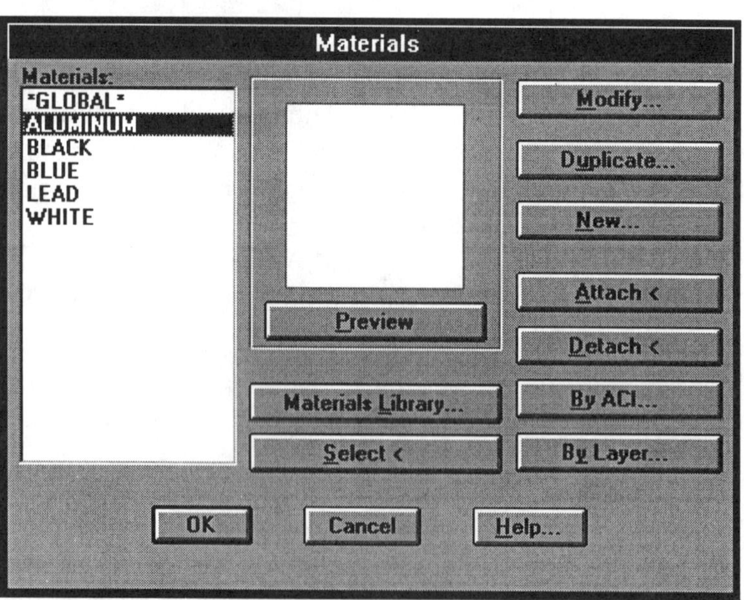

The following is the procedure to access and attach a material.

1. Use the RMAT command to display the Materials dialog box.

2. If materials were already included in the drawing, you could select them from the Materials list on the left side of the Materials dialog box. But if the drawing is new, you will need to import materials into the drawing. This is accomplished by picking the Materials Library Button. You are presented with the Materials Library dialog box shown in Figure 7.18.

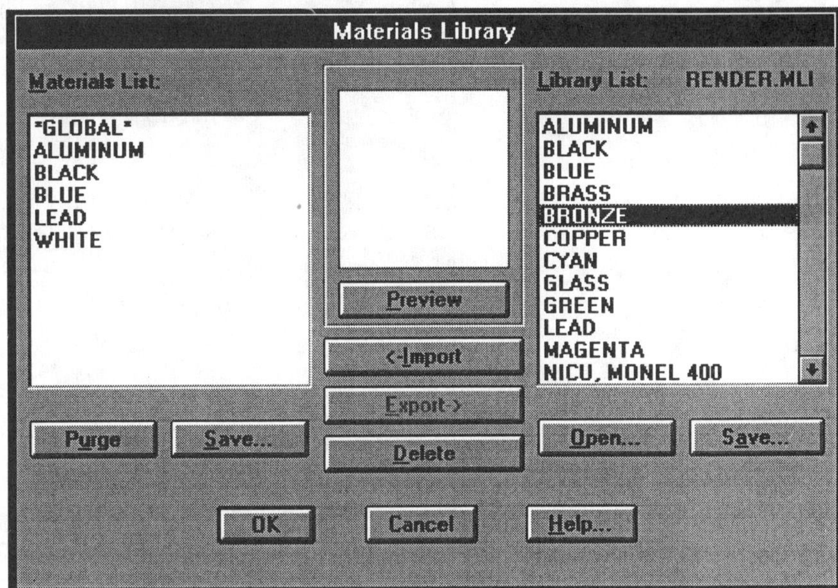

Figure 7.18
Materials Library dialog box

3. Along the right side of the box is the Library list. Normally it displays the default library - RENDER.MLI. You can scroll through the list and highlight the desired materials to bring into your drawing. When you have highlighted the ones you want, pick the Import button and these materials are brought over into your drawing.

4. You can preview any single material that you highlight, either from the Materials list or the Library list.

5. You can save a drawing's Material list to its own library by using the Save button. It allows you to create a library file with the extension .MLI. You can then use this list in other drawings by opening it as a library.

6. Once you have created your materials list, use the OK button to return to the Materials dialog box.

7. Then, highlight the material you want to assign and pick either the Attach, By ACI, or the By Layer buttons. The Attach button allows

you to attach the material to a specific object. The By ACI button allows you to assign a material to a color in the drawing. The By Layer button allows you to assign a material to a specific layer.

8. If you select the Modify or New button, you are presented with a dialog box similar to Figure 7.19. This allows you to create your own materials or to modify existing ones.

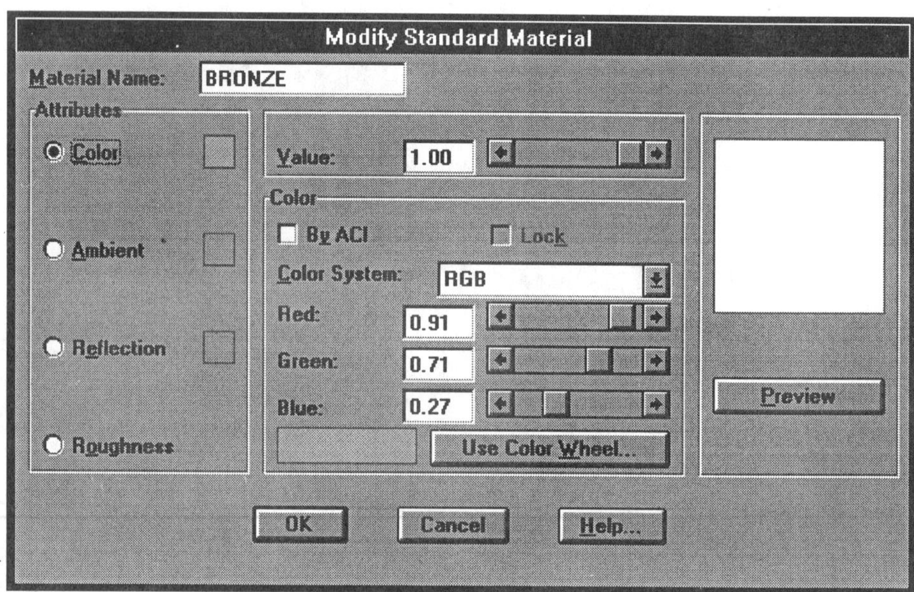

Figure 7.19
Modify Standard Material
dialog box

7.14 RENDER and Rendering Preferences

The Render and Rendering Preferences dialog boxes have been altered to add the new options. The Rendering Preferences dialog box pre-sets the rendering conditions.

Rendering Preferences

By making use of the options in the Rendering Preferences dialog box, you can control the rendering speed, destination, edge smoothness, applied finishes, and more. These are default values to help speed up the rendering process. Settings subject to constant use should be recorded here. Refer to Figure 7.20 for the Rendering Preferences dialog box. The following lists some of the options available.

- The Smooth Shading option blends edges together to give a curved surface a smooth appearance. You can specify the maximum included angle for adjoining surfaces that you wish to smooth.

- The Apply Materials option toggles on and off the application of preset materials to the model.

- The More Options button presents you with the dialog box shown in Figure 7.21. Gouraud shading is the quicker of the Rendering Qualities, while Phong gives a higher degree of rendering by calculating every pixel on the rendering screen.

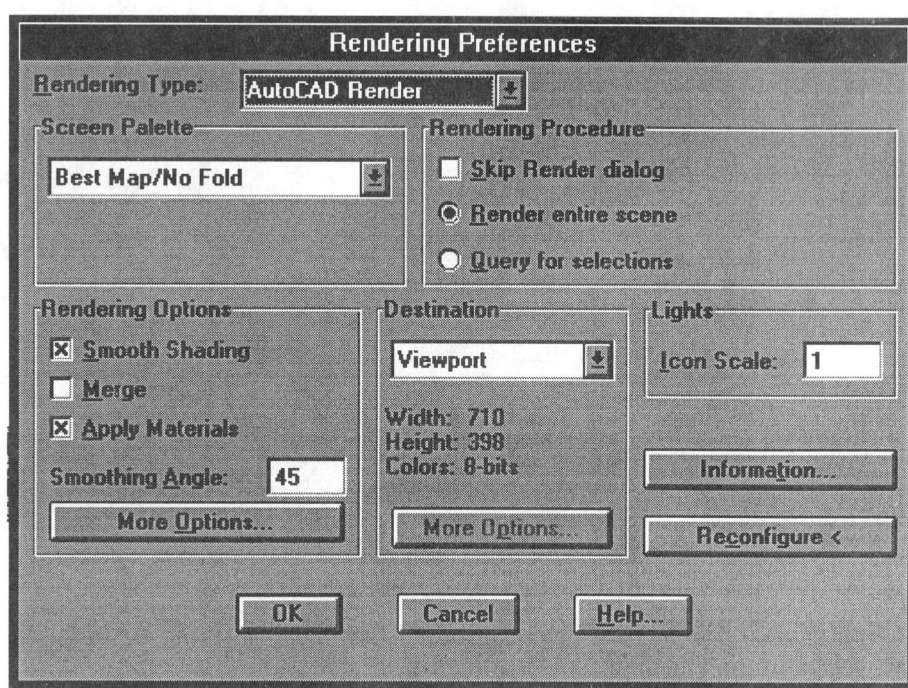

Figure 7.20
Rendering Preferences dialog box

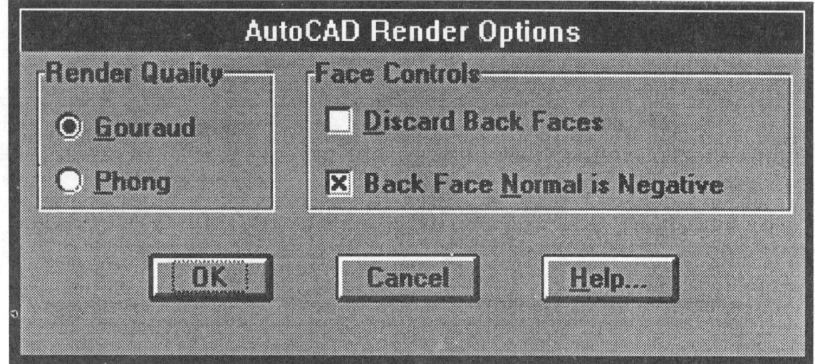

Figure 7.21
AutoCAD Render Options subdialog box

Rendering the Model

The RENDER command will render a selected scene or the current display if no scene is selected. Refer to Figure 7.22 for the Render dialog box. The rendering will either fill the screen or fit within an active viewport, or in the case of the Windows version, be displayed in the Render window, depending on the settings of the Render dialog box.

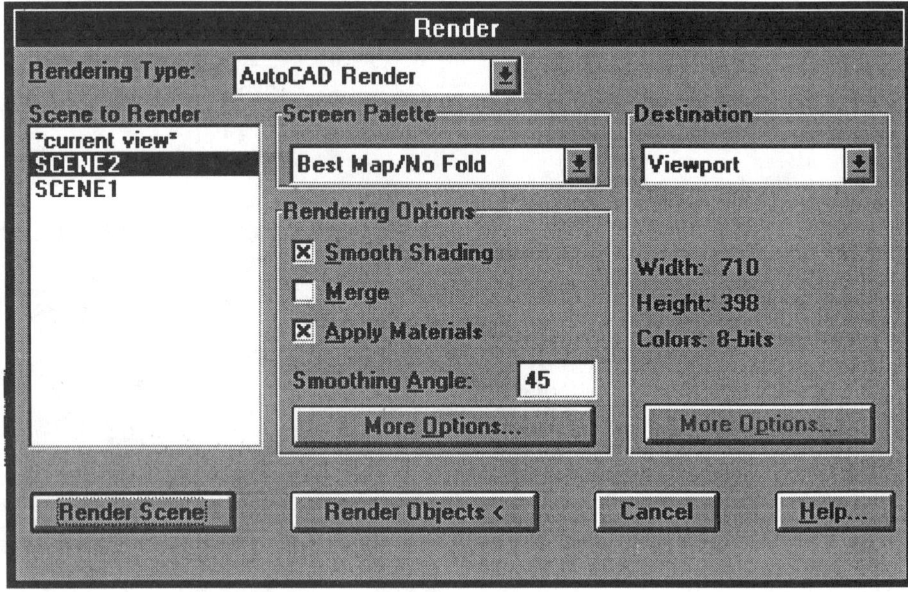

If the rendering fills the screen and you want to return to the AutoCAD graphics screen, press the space bar. The image is still in the Framebuffer, so you can save it using the SAVEIMG command.

Once the image is rendered, you can save the image to an external file so that you may replay it at another time. To save an image, use the SAVEIMG command (Refer to Figure 7.23); to replay an image, use the REPLAY command (Refer to Figure 7.24.)

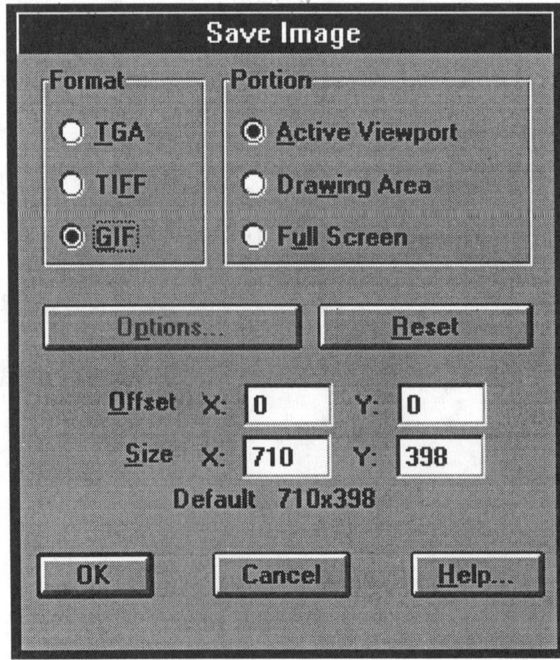

You can save the image in different graphic forms depending on the type of graphics card the system contains. GIF files are usually the smallest, whereas the others contain more information and occupy more space. If the image is displayed in the Render window, the image may be saved as a BMP file.

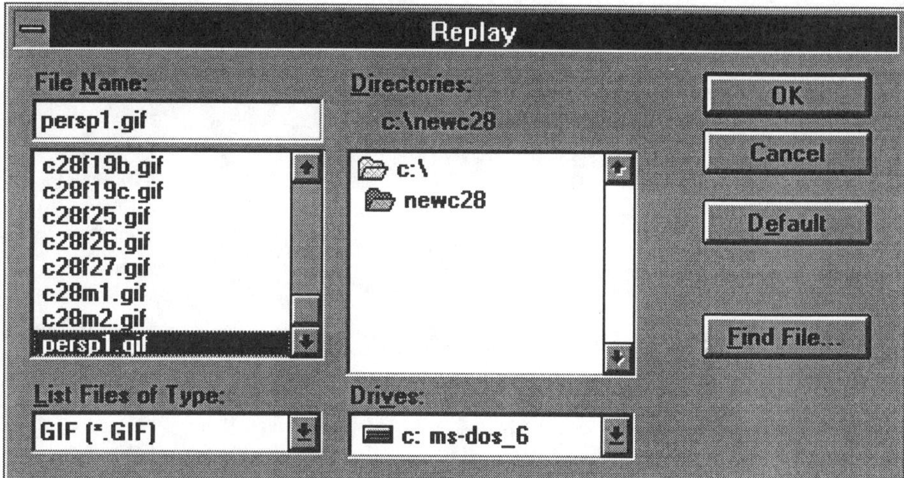

Figure 7.24
Replay dialog box

Index